# *The Threat Hunt Process (THP) Roadmap*

### *A Pathway for Advanced Cybersecurity Active Measures*

**Mark A. Russo**, CISSP-ISSAP, CEH

*Former Chief Information Security Officer (CISO), Department of Education*

Syber-Risk

## DEDICATION

*This book is dedicated to the cyber-security men and women of the Department of Defense (DOD) and the United States Cybercommand (US Cybercommand) that protect and defend the Information Systems of this great Nation.*

*This is also dedicated to my family who have been supportive of my endeavors to plunge into writing as not just a hobby but a calling to make the world a better and more secure place.*

Syber-Risk

# On September 1, 2018 we launched the _Most Extensive_ Cybersecurity Blog Site

*This is the major resource of everything "Cyber."*
*"The good, the bad, and the ugly of cybersecurity all in one place."*

Join us at https://cybersentinel.tech

*This free resource is available to everyone interested in the fate and future of cybersecurity in the 21st Century*

ALSO SEE THE AUTHOR'S EBOOK: *Huawei Technologies: Chinese Risk to the International Supply Chain* at: _https://cybersentinel.tech/product/ebook-huawei-technologies-chinese-risk-to-the-international-supply-chain/_

# The Threat Hunt Process (THP) Roadmap

## Table of Contents

**PART I - The Strategic View of the Threat Hunt Process (THP)**

# Introduction

The Cybersecurity Threat Hunting Process (THP) is an *active* and coordinated effort between the Incident Response (IR) and the Cyber Threat Intelligence (CTI) teams. It is not OFFENSIVE and is specifically used to confirm whether an *occurrence* becomes an *event.* Based upon available intelligence, an event may or may not be raised to a defined *incident*. The IR team will determine whether the event should be raised to an actual incident for timely and actual response activities working with CTI. The IR team may or may not direct a **hunt** be initiated and will make that determination based on the potential or actual level of risk posed by the intrusion.

---

## EVENT → INCIDENT
**(less defined/initial occurrence) → (defined/confirmed/high impact)**

---

The *Incident Response Spectrum* describes the major activities that the IR team may implement—the offense, or a hack-back is seldom authorized or recommended against the threat[1] of each part of the spectrum as found below. THP coordinates its actions with the IR team, reviews the available Cybersecurity Threat Intelligence (CTI), and works with system administrators, coders, and forensics analysts to locate, mitigate, and stop any malicious activities. THP is that first-line of defense by internal experts to respond rapidly to threats to the Information Technology (IT) environment.

---

[1] A **Hack-back** is not recommended. Actions, especially against nation-state hackers, may result in far more damage by the hacker than initiating an attack against the threat target. The best course of action is determining the attribution of the attackers and reporting as part of an established Incident Response Plan (IRP) to authorities.

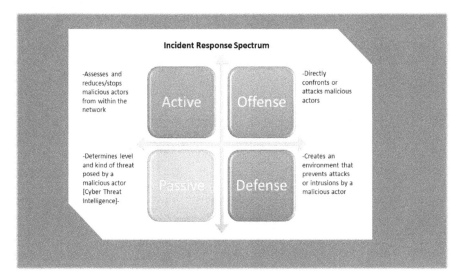

The Threat Hunting Process (THP) may be used by both public agencies and private companies. This is a resource intensive operation, and typically is sought by medium and large size companies needing to protect its information, sensitive data, Intellectual Property or government data from unauthorized access. The THP further defines how the hunting process functions and interacts with other functions and processes. These processes provide Cybersecurity Analysts (CyA), both within the CTI and Hunt teams, with a method to identify malicious activity throughout the operational IT environment.

Major elements of THP are identified below in Graphic 1. This provides a high-level overview of the various cybersecurity functions with a specific emphasis on the Hunt process.

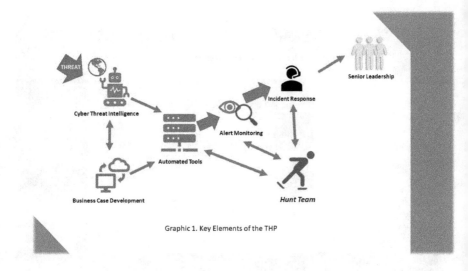

Graphic 1. Key Elements of the THP

The process provides high-confidence, repeatability, and identification of both cybersecurity events and incidents. The business case development process provides feedback to the THP to improve incident response personnel actions with a defined capability to conduct follow-on responses and forensic activities. The THP receives inputs primarily[2] from the following four areas:

1. **Cyber Threat Intelligence (CTI)**

2. **Automated Tool**

3. **Business Case Development**

4. **Incident Response (IR)**

These inputs generate new hunt scenarios and provide feedback to incident response personnel. These responses leverage the available intelligence and further assists in ongoing analysis and forensic activities. These areas provide the needed information for successful hunt team operations and outcomes.

Both the manual and automated continuous monitoring applications and devices are critical to THP success. *Continuous Monitoring* (ConMon) is an integral component of an effective implementation of the National Institute for Standards and Technology's (NIST)

---

[2] Other inputs may include information from public alert websites/feeds and the federal government specific to their role or industry.

Risk Management Framework (RMF). ConMon provides the next evolution in true progress within the realm of cybersecurity; it has yet to be achieved by most companies and agencies. See Appendix B, *Continuous Monitoring's Importance to the THP*, for a deeper discussion of the role of ConMon and its direct support to the THP.

## *What is Risk?*

Risk is a crucial concern by key leaders and should be understood to make resourcing decisions to support the THP. While threats are focused on the inbound dangers such as nation-state hackers, insider threats, etc., risk is focused on the potentialities of loss or harm to the organization. Risk, if properly applied, helps senior leaders make critical decisions of how much and where to focus limited resources against a threat—specific or broadly.

| Risk | Threat |
|---|---|
| *Definition* | *Definition* |
| A measure of the extent to which an entity is threatened by a potential circumstance or event, and typically a function of: (i) the adverse impacts that would arise if the circumstance or event occurs; and (ii) the likelihood of occurrence. Information system-related security risks are those risks that arise from the loss of confidentiality, integrity, or availability of information or information systems and reflect the potential adverse impacts to organizational operations (including mission, functions, image, or reputation), organizational assets, individuals, other organizations, and the Nation. | Any circumstance or event with the potential to adversely impact organizational operations (including mission, functions, image, or reputation), organizational assets, individuals, other organizations, or the Nation through an information system via unauthorized access, destruction, disclosure, modification of information, and/or denial of service. |

Also, many will confuse risk with threat and use the terms interchangeably. A threat, be it an intentional threat such as a hacker, or natural disaster, is a subset of risk. The Risk Management Framework (RMF) created by NIST is based on active knowledge, recognition, and a plan to address by the business or agency to provide a reportable and repeatable mechanism that creates the real success of the concept of "risk management." This is not "risk elimination;" it is about an active means to manage risk, and any associated threats over time. The standard cybersecurity equation for risk can be computed as following:

RISK = Threat  X  Vulnerability  X Consequence

*The Three Elements of Risk*

## The Difference Between an 'Event' and an 'Incident'

*Incident Response (IR) primarily requires a plan. It also requires the identification of who or what agency is notified when a breach has occurred.*

The first effort should be identifying with, for example, government representatives what constitutes a reportable event that formally becomes an **incident**. This could include a confirmed breach that has occurred to the IT infrastructure. Incidents could include anything from a Denial of Service (DOS) attack—an overloading of outwardly facing web or mail servers-- or exfiltration of data—where Controlled Unclassified Information (CUI) data has been copied or moved to outside of the organization's firewall/perimeter. Incidents could also include the destruction of data that, for example, is identified through ongoing audit activities.

Secondarily, who do you notify? Do you alert, for example, an assigned Contract Officer Representative (COR), the Contract Office itself, DOD's US Cybercommand at Fort Meade, MD, or possibly the Department of Homeland Security's (DHS) Computer Emergency Response Team (CERT) (https://www.us-cert.gov/forms/report)? Cybersecurity personnel and senior leaders will have to ask where to file standard government "incident" reports. These organizations should be able to provide templates and forms specific to the agency's own unique reporting requirements.

IR requires the testing of IR Plan (IRP) at least ***annually***. However, it is suggested that organization's test more often. Until comfortable with the IR "reporting chain," ***practice, practice, practice***.

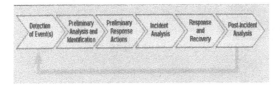

**The DOD Cyber Incident Life Cycle.** This diagram from the DOD is a representative example of a typical "incident response life cycle." It is intended to assist in IR activities, and will better assist in coordination with government cybersecurity incident response organizations. Recognizing this as either an "event" (not necessarily a negative occurrence) versus an "incident" is an internal determination by the leadership in coordination with its cybersecurity and IT professional staffs to include the hunt team. An incident specifically requires alerting the government as soon as the intrusion is *recognized*.

Verify with the respective agency its reporting standards. Typically, **events** may not need to be reported based on the expansive impacts and workloads to especially government cybersecurity response organizations. In the case of **incidents**, the standard is 72-hours to submit a report; however, the recommendation is *as soon as possible* due to the potential impacts beyond the IT infrastructure. Furthermore, it can pose a serious direct threat to interconnected federal agency IT environments.

The chart below categorizes current Department of Defense (DOD) and Department of Homeland Security (DHS) common precedence designations. It provides both a standard categorization for identified events and typically, precedence is used to identify the level of action and response depending on the precedence "severity."

| Precedence | Category | Description |
|---|---|---|
| 0 | 0 | Training and Exercises |
| 1 | 1 | Root Level Intrusion (Incident) |
| 2 | 2 | User Level Intrusion (Incident) |
| 3 | 4 | Denial of Service (Incident) |
| 4 | 7 | Malicious Logic (Incident) |
| 5 | 3 | Unsuccessful Activity Attempt (Event) |
| 6 | 5 | Non-Compliance Activity (Event) |
| 7 | 6 | Reconnaissance (Event) |
| 8 | 8 | Investigating (Event) |
| 9 | 9 | Explained Anomaly (Event) |

**DOD Precedence Categorization.** Nine (9) is the lowest event where little is known, and IT personnel are attempting to determine whether this activity should be elevated to alert leadership or to "close it out." One (1) is a deep attack. It identifies that the incident has gained "root" access. Root access can be construed as that the intruder has complete access to the most restrictive security levels of a system. This type of access usually is interpreted to be complete and unfettered access to networks and data. (SOURCE: Cyber Incident Handling Program, CJCSM 6510.01B, 18 December 2014, http://www.jcs.mil/Portals/36/Documents/Library/Manuals/m651001.pdf?ver=2016-02-05-175710-897)

# The Threat is China

No discussion of THP would be complete without some discussion of the major nation-state actors that pose a daily threat to the global community. While Russia, Iran, and North Korea or known active attackers, China poses the main threat for the foreseeable future. China considers the use of an assassin's mace the key to its worldwide dominance. Cybersecurity exploitation is seen by the Chinese's as a key element of its asymmetric "warfare" against the West. (I recommend reading the book, *The Hundred-Year Marathon*, by Michael Pillsbury to provide a much more expansive understanding of China's long-game strategy).

In February 2015, the Director of National Intelligence (DNI), identified one of the major risks facing the United States (US) within the "Cyber" domain is the insertion of malicious code into Information Technology (IT) hardware and software items sold to the US. According to the DNI: "Despite ever-improving network defenses, the diverse possibilities for...supply chain operations to insert compromised hardware or software...will hold nearly all [Information and Communication Technology] systems at risk for years to come" (DNI, 2015, p.1).

While there are several foreign IT equipment and software companies that have been accused of such activities, the major threat in this arena is the Chinese company *Huawei (Wah-way) Technologies Company, Limited*. In 2012, the House Permanent Select Committee on Intelligence had major concerns. Specific to its investigation of the operating practices of Huawei, the committee reported that: "The threat posed [by Huawei/China] to U.S. national-security interests... in the telecommunications supply chain is an increasing priority..." (US House of Representatives, 2012, p.1).

While there are no specific unclassified details of such injections of malicious code into Huawei products, in 2006, for example, a discreet ban by several Western nations, to include the US, was initiated against the Chinese firm of **Lenovo** Personal Computers. Shortly after Lenovo purchased International Business Machine's (IBM) personal computing division, the use or purchase of Lenovo PCs "...due to backdoor vulnerabilities" (Infosec Institute, 2013) was banned.

Huawei represents a similar and more pervasive threat to the international IT supply chain. Huawei has both the means and motives to compromise IT equipment and systems on the behalf of the Chinese government. "...Huawei has refused to explain its relationship with the Chinese government or the role of the Communist Party...inside the company..." (Simonite, 2012), and it can be assumed, based on multiple Huawei senior leaders with close ties with the People's Liberation Army (PLA) that Huawei has an explicit connection with the Chinese government.

The major motivation for Huawei, as a surrogate for the Chinese government, is to support its 5-year Plan focused on it becoming a major global economic super-power. Huawei is implicitly aligned with this plan that "State-owned enterprises are instructed to acquire assets perceived as valuable by Beijing" (Scissors, 2013 ). It continues a wide-range of acquisitions to include mergers with American and other Western IT companies.

The PLA's Unit 61398 has been extensively analyzed by government and private cybersecurity firms. In 2013, **Mandiant** released an exhaustive and authoritative report based upon deep-analysis of code and techniques specific to Unit 61398. The most conclusive statement made was that the "...Communist Party of China is tasking the Chinese People's Liberation Army [Unit 61398 and others] to commit systematic cyber-espionage and data theft..." (Mandiant, 2013, p. 7). It can be further agreed that some of that training, equipment and expertise is provided by Huawei directly to the PLA. The **Far Eastern Economic Review** reported "...Huawei received a key contract to supply the PLA's first national telecommunications network" (Ahrens, 2013). These ties point to connections with the Chinese government and the PLA; there is little doubt that China continues aggressive cyber-activities in support of its intentions to increase its economic standing in the world.

China has not demonstrated a desire to quash cyber-espionage activities from within its borders. It can be surmised that many Chinese cyber-activities are supported and controlled under the auspices of the Chinese government. The most lucrative target for China, and more specifically Huawei, is the US; it will continue to focus its vast resources against US economic and business entities.

Additionally, Huawei has multiple cyber-relevant capabilities to include hardware and software development, IT manufacturing, and in-house technical expertise. However, the major capability afforded Huawei is through its direct backing by the Chinese government. As noted, in terms of government contracts and resources Huawei has powerful direct support.

In terms of its infrastructure, it is vast and vibrant. Access to the Internet as a surreptitious mechanism to hide its activities is another potential threat posed by Huawei to subvert the worlds' IT architecture. By leveraging its own internal infrastructure, in conjunction with the Chinese state, it has near limitless capabilities to disrupt the US and its allies via the Internet.

According to Lachow, Huawei as a complex agent, would require "...a team of individuals (or perhaps multiple teams) with expertise in a number of technical areas..." (Lachow, 2008, p. 444). Huawei, in coordination with the PLA (or vice versa), has access to such formidable resources; "[t]he PLA is reaching out across a wide swath of [the] Chinese civilian sector to meet the intensive requirements necessary to support its burgeoning [Information Warfare] capabilities, incorporating people with specialized skills from commercial industry..." (Krekel, 2009, p. 7).

Huawei should be expected to mostly use the Internet for passive cyber-espionage collection activities; however, it has the potential to engage in more active operations. This could include establishing secretive Command and Control (C2) nodes within its own sold equipment and software, and also in "infected" competitors' equipment sold in the international marketplace. With this access, it could pose a formidable offensive capability. Huawei has a huge target-set to pursue. With its growth throughout the global IT marketplace, any nation requiring IT products offers a target-rich environment for Huawei to exploit. Targets available to Huawei are wide-ranging and span the entire developed and industrial nations that conduct regular business with Huawei.

All countries are potentially exploitable especially in terms of their reliance on the Internet. The need for computer hardware and software by all developed nations affords a consistent and regular vulnerability. It can be surmised that Huawei personnel have the requisite knowledge and ability to exploit all levels of its manufactured products (and those of its competitors); this capability provides a direct ability to align with Beijing's motivations to become the predominant economic powerhouse of the world.

In terms of cyber-espionage, the magnitude is greater than $445 B annually "...to the world economy" (Nakashima & Peterson, 2014) as identified in a 2014 *Washington Post* article. If the allegations against Huawei are true, the potential economic loss to the world could be far greater if Huawei has expanded capacity to process the volumes of exfiltrated data. The graver implications would be damage to the global economy more in the trillions of dollars annually in stolen intellectual property and data.

The severest, and more exploitive consequence would be Huawei could have the ability to leverage injected malicious code in its products. This would imply the ability to shutdown portions or the entire Internet because of its control of foundational backbone hardware devices such as routers, switches, and firewalls. While the ongoing cyber-espionage economic losses to countries are serious, it has the potential to inflict massive offensive harm against countries or groups that in the future it may be in conflict to include the US.

## Conclusion

Huawei is a *complex* threat. Lachow reserves this label to highly coordinated and effective state actors with nearly unlimited resources. Huawei is such a threat with the obligatory skill-sets to a very diverse and technologically capable adversary. With the presumptive backing of the Chinese government, and its resources, Huawei continues to be a major threat to US and international governments and their respective economies.

While there is no conclusive or public evidence, that China through its surrogate Huawei has injected malicious coding into any of its products, the risk is formidable. Michael Maloof, a former senior security policy analyst in the Office of the Secretary of Defense, ascribes from sources that "[t]he Chinese government reportedly has "pervasive access" to some 80 percent of the world's communications, thanks to backdoors it has ordered to be installed in devices made by Huawei" (Protalinski, 2012). Jim Lewis, at the Center for Strategic and International Studies provides an ominous point of view working with Chinese businesses: "The Chinese will tell you that stealing technology and business secrets [are] a way of building their economy, and that this is important for national security" (Metz, 2013). The risk to the US's national security, its economic viability, and its critical infrastructure is directly threatened by the Chinese regime.

# References for "The Threat is China"

Ahrens, N. (2013, February). *China's Competitiveness: Myth, Reality and Lessons for the United States and Japan*. Retrieved from Center for Strategic and International Studies: http://csis.org/files/publication/130215_competitiveness_Huawei_casestudy_Web.pdf

Barbozaaug, D. (2010, August 22). *Scrutiny for Chinese Telecom Bid*. Retrieved from New York Times: http://www.nytimes.com/2010/08/23/business/global/23telecom.html?_r=0

DNI. (2015, February 26). *Statement of Record: Worldwide Threat Assessment*. Retrieved from http://www.armed-services.senate.gov/imo/media/doc/Stewart_02-26-15.pdf

Infosec Institute. (2013, October 11). *Hardware attacks, backdoors and electronic component qualification*. Retrieved from Infosec Institute: http://resources.infosecinstitute.com/hardware-attacks-backdoors-and-electronic-component-qualification/

Krekel, B. (2009, October 9). *Capability of the People's Republic of China to Conduct Cyber Warfare and Computer Network Exploitation*. Retrieved from George Washington University: http://nsarchive.gwu.edu/NSAEBB/NSAEBB424/docs/Cyber-030.pdf

Lachow, I. (2008). Cyber Terrorism: Menace or Myth. *Cyber Power*, 19-20.

Mandiant. (2013, February 18). *APT1: Exposing One of China's Cyber Espionage Units*. Retrieved from Mandiant: http://intelreport.mandiant.com/Mandiant_APT1_Report.pdf

Metz, C. (2013, December 31). *U.S. to China: We Hacked Your Internet Gear We Told You Not to Hack*. Retrieved from Wired: http://www.wired.com/2013/12/nsa-cisco-huawei-china/

Nakashima, E., & Peterson, A. (2014, June 9). *Report: Cybercrime and espionage costs $445 billion annually*. Retrieved from Washington Post: http://www.washingtonpost.com/world/national-security/report-cybercrime-and-espionage-costs-445-billion-annually/2014/06/08/8995291c-ecce-11e3-9f5c-9075d5508f0a_story.html

Protalinski, E. (2012, July 14). *Former Pentagon analyst: China has backdoors to 80% of telecoms*. Retrieved from ZDNet: http://www.zdnet.com/article/former-pentagon-analyst-china-has-backdoors-to-80-of-telecoms/

Scissors, D. P. (2013 , May 9). *Chinese Investment in the U.S.: Facts and Motives*. Retrieved from Heritage Society: http://www.heritage.org/research/testimony/2013/05/chinese-investment-in-the-us-facts-and-motives

Simonite, T. (2012, October 9). *Why the United States Is So Afraid of Huawei*. Retrieved from MIT Technology Review: http://www.technologyreview.com/news/429542/why-the-united-states-is-so-afraid-of-huawei/

US House of Representatives. (2012, October 8). *Investigative Report on the US National Security Issues Posed by Chinese Telecommunications Companies Huawei and ZTE*. Retrieved from https://intelligence.house.gov/sites/intelligence.house.gov/files/documents/Huawei-ZTE%20Investigative%20Report%20(FINAL).pdf

## The Threat Hunt Process

"Hunts" follow the process outlined below. This ensures that all hunts provide feedback and value to the company, business, or agency. They require a consistent and repeatable response. The THP also requires "continual improvement" element like many mainstream development processes such as the Information Technology Information Library® (ITIL). Continual improvement requires, for example, after-action meetings, training, and outside third-party evaluation on a recurring basis; these are but several measures designed to improve the organizations' cybersecurity threat response activities and capabilities.

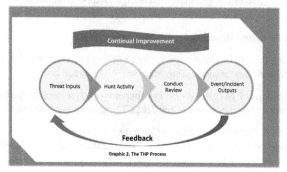

Graphic 2. The THP Process

### Threat Inputs

Cybersecurity Analysts (CyA) will begin hunts based on received **hunt requests[3]** or **base hunts** from the Incident Response Team and generated by a developed **Master Hunt Tracking Database (MHTDB)**. The MHTDB is a defined repository that tracks Indicators of Compromise (IOC) that assist in determining who and what level of attack is deployed based upon such indicators,

---

[3] **Hunt** requests are typically triggered by outside detected events and **base hunts** are used to assess organizational and individual compliance with Acceptable Use Policies (AUP) covering organizational personnel.

intelligence, patterns of attack, etc., that assists in formulating a better understanding of threat capabilities and motivations within the target IT environment. IOCs may be developed from internal experts, but there are several low-cost and no-cost solutions already developed for the public and private sectors use for their companies and agencies.

These include:

1. FireEyes's ® publicly shared IOC's of Github at: https://github.com/fireeye/iocs
2. The DHS shares Joint Indicator Bulletins at: https://www.us-cert.gov/ncas/bulletins
3. DHS also offers Automated Indicator Sharing (AIS). More information on how to integrate with these services may be found at: https://www.dhs.gov/ais
4. Crowdstrike® also offers IOC access via its Falcon Query API. More information can be found at: https://www.crowdstrike.com/blog/tech-center/import-iocs-crowdstrike-falcon-host-platform-via-api/
5. Also, work being done in Artificial Intelligence (AI) by the company Cylance® is also providing cutting-edge approaches for end-point protection. See www.cylance.com

## Hunt Activity

Hunt requests may originate from the following three functional areas; however, final determination for the action is the responsibility of the IR team (based on the immediacy, it may also be in coordination with senior management for alert and visibility purposes).

1. Cyber Threat Intelligence (CTI) – Internally/externally sourced CTI including operational Communities of Interest (CoI), Government Partners, Law Enforcement, etc. Based upon CTI review of the available intelligence, it may "tip" a potential hunt activity to IR for action.

2. Business Case Development – Feedback on a **rule creation**[4] request is received by the business case development process. Here it is determined whether the following applies:

   a) A historical hunt should be performed in addition to the development of a new business case.

   b) It would not be feasible to create an automated rule for the request, and a

---

[4] **Rule creation** can be either applied in a manual manner by a CyA or more likely as a "rule" implemented within automated security devices to include firewalls, Intrusion Prevention Systems (IPS), or Security Information Event Management (SIEM) devices.

manual hunt should be initiated to better refine the business case of the identified threat. *Is more information needed to provide a fuller picture of the threat?*

**3. Incident Response** – Indicators of Compromise (IOC) provided by the CTI or like external organization has identified a potential threat vector or actual attack. IR will direct hunt resources as appropriate to initiate a hunt. *This is the primary source and de facto leader over the THP.*

## Hunt

Hunts are typically focused against external attackers but may also include "insider threat" activities. Using the inputs, a CyA will initiate a THP activity/hunt upon direction. The hunt consists of selecting the proper tools to use, collecting the data from the tools, analyzing the results, and documenting the outcomes. CyA perform an iterative process by querying the selected tools, reviewing the data, filtering out known or non-malicious behavior and re-querying the data. This continues until malicious activities are found. Analysts will make use of either existing tools, or by creation or procurement of new tools to fulfill the needs of the hunt. Gaps in tool capabilities should be documented and reviewed by corporate or agency leadership. This may include Senior IR Personnel or specialized experts to include the assigned Chief Information Security Officer (CISO).

## Base Hunts

Base hunts are typically internally focused on **matters of compliance** from within the IT environment. It is defined as repeatable searches based on an analytical methodology that produces low-fidelity results (i.e., results that require analyst review and cannot be fully automated as a rule). These hunts will reside in the MHTDB. Base hunts, for example, may leverage tools such as FireEye HX® technology; this technology obtains endpoint intelligence that may include, but is not limited to, Windows Services listing, Windows Scheduled Task listing, Windows Registry Run keys, and the Windows Application Compatibility Cache. The tool will help to determine whether any alteration or manipulation of these key services and may lead to follow-on review and correction by trained personnel.

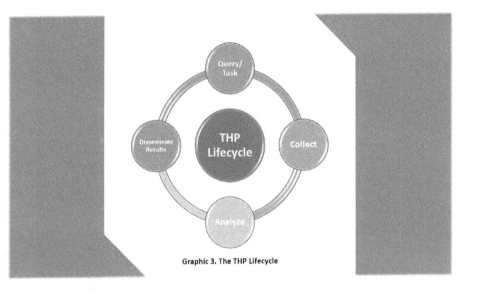

Graphic 3. The THP Lifecycle

Upon completion of a review of the data, analysts will document the outcomes of their findings.

## Outcomes
All hunts will end in one of three outcomes. Based on the outcome of the hunt, an analyst will document the results accordingly and distribute to other functions and processes as necessary.

### 1. Nothing Discovered
No indication of active compromise or behavior violating identified best practices, acceptable use, or organizational policies discovered during the hunt.

### 2. Something Found: Non-Malicious
Violation(s) of acceptable use or organizational policy discovered during the hunt.

### 3. Something Found: Malicious
An active or historic compromise, which may currently or have previously placed, IT assets, or its data at risk, is discovered.

## Conduct Review

*To ensure that the hunt team's analysts remain focused on relevant and important hunts, analysts must evaluate completed hunts and move all hunts possible to the business case development.*

### Should the hunt become a base hunt?

Does the analyst believe the logic utilized provides repeatable and low-fidelity results that serve as a good starting point for future hunts, the logic used should be documented in the MHTDB? Is the malicious actor from within the organization or has unique access? This would warrant initiating a follow-on base hunt for active or potential follow-on intrusions requiring continual monitoring.

### Can the hunt become a rule?

If an analyst determines that a hunt may become a rule, documentation of the hunt should be delivered to the business case development process. The information should be formulated into a rule that can be applied to monitoring and alert devices[5] on the network. This too should be transferred to the MHTDB. The hunt team is responsible for documenting the methodology followed within the MHTDB and providing this information to the business case process personnel.

### Is the hunt effective?

Hunts may lose their effectiveness over time, and a determination of focusing resources on an activity may divert from other important hunt priorities. There are several reasons a hunt may lose its effectiveness or further need to be pursued:

- Creation of a rule covering the same activity set may address the threat
- Completed patching against a known vulnerability may partially or totally mitigate the need for the hunt
- Improved automated tools or policies may also mitigate the threat
- Determination that the hunted activity no longer presents a threat

Hunting can consume a significant amount of time, and analysts must ensure that their resources remain focused on real and active threats. Whenever a CyA determines

---

[5] "Smart" network devices may include firewalls, Intrusion Detection/Prevention Systems, or Security Incident Event Monitoring (SIEM) hardware.

that a hunt can no longer provide effective results, documentation of the reasoning must be included in the MHTDB for the retirement of the hunt.

## Event/Incident Outputs

Based on the outcome of the hunt, an analyst will document the results within the MHTDB. The outcomes (reports) will be distributed as inputs to the IR function or business case development processes and provide necessary feedback to improve the analytical reports provided by the CTI function.

### Incident Response
If the hunt began from information collected from an IR function, providing feedback to that team helps improve its output. The IR team will be notified immediately following the verification of a malicious event in an information system or network.

### Business Case Development
Upon determination that a high-fidelity, repeatable search has been found to be effective in detecting anomalous or malicious activity, the logic will be delivered to the business case development process for creating or modifying current automated rules.

### Cyber Threat Intelligence (CTI)
If the hunt began from information collected from the CTI function, providing feedback to that team helps improve their analysis. The hunt process provides feedback relative to the provided intelligence including the results of the hunt. It also supports the hunt by determining whether additional information is required to continue, and whether any information gained from the hunt could lead to additional and useable intelligence. Any such additional intelligence would directly contribute to the value and improvement of a CTI intelligence product or report.

## THP Decision Tree Activities

*Hunt Request (Externally-focused)*: A pure hunt request is typically focused on outside threats that have been detected or anticipated based upon IOCs. This includes actual threats to operations within the agency's IT environment.

The following flowchart shows the *hunt request* workflow.

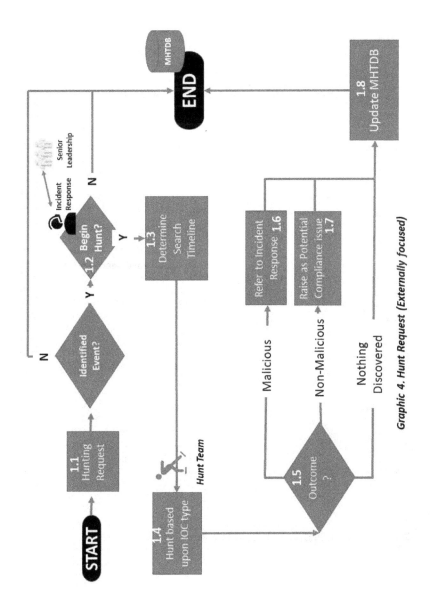

*Graphic 4. Hunt Request (Externally focused)*

# Roadmap Details

*Hunt – Responsibility-Accountability-Consulted-Information (RACI) Matrix*

| 1.1 | | | Hunt Request |
|---|---|---|---|
| **Input** | | | Trigger Events: One of the following reactive or proactive triggers will prompt the initiation of the hunt request process:<br><br>• **Cyber Threat Intelligence:** IOCs provided by the CTI function whether internally/externally sourced, include, for example, Communities of Interest (CoI), Government Partners, Law Enforcement, etc.<br><br>• **Business Case Development:** Feedback on a rule creation request received by the business case development process where it is determined that a hunt would be appropriate based upon input.<br><br>• **Incident Response:** IOCs provided by an IR function as part of, or resulting from, incident response activities. |
| **RACI** | R | Hunt Team | Responsible for analyzing the hunt request and determining whether appropriate details have been received to evaluate the request. |
| | A | Hunt Team Lead | Accountable to ensure that the hunt request is given proper consideration and analysis. |
| | C | Trigger Source(s) | Consulted to provide detailed context regarding the hunt. |
| | I | Trigger Source(s) | Informed of the next stage of analysis. |
| **Details** | | | Hunt teams analyze a hunt request made by the trigger source(s) and determines if there is appropriate information to evaluate the hunt request. |
| **Output** | | | Hunt request requiring evaluation |

| 1.2 | | Begin Hunt? |
|---|---|---|
| **Input** | | Hunt request requiring evaluation |
| **RACI** | **R** Hunt Team | Responsible for analyzing the hunt request and determining whether to initiate a hunt. |
| | **A** Hunt Team Lead | Accountable to ensure that the hunt request is given proper consideration and analysis. |
| | **C** Trigger Source(s) | Consulted to provide detailed context regarding the hunt. |
| | **I** Trigger Source(s) | Informed of the next stage of analysis. |
| **Details** | | The hunt team evaluates the hunt request and better determines whether to initiate a hunt in coordination with IR personnel. The following criteria are used to determine if a hunt is to be initiated immediately or if further evaluation is required from an input source: |

**Cyber Threat Intelligence**

*Watchlists*

The CTI team maintains access to various sources of intelligence feeds that provide high-confidence for identified IOCs. Current whitelisted sources include, for example, iSight Threat Intelligence®.

The hunt team initiates a hunt based upon indicators received from a threat intelligence source. (*Again, in coordination and at the direction of the IR team*).

*IOC - Recommendation to Hunt*

The CTI function will provide IOCs to the hunt team and issue a recommendation to hunt when a moderate-to-high level of analyst confidence is obtained.

*IOC – No Recommendation to Hunt*

The CTI function will periodically provide IOCs to the hunt team that do not include a recommendation to hunt when a low-to-moderate level of analyst confidence is obtained.

The hunt team performs further evaluation when an IOC with no recommendation to hunt is received from the CTI function.

### Business Case Development

The business case development function may periodically provide IOCs and complementary courses of action to the hunt team. This may result in new rule request development effort. This is based upon recommendation and approval by the IR team where the business case (use case) development function deems a hunt may be appropriate.

The hunt team performs further evaluation when an IOC hunt suggestion is received.

### Incident Response

The IR function may direct an IOC hunt as part of, or resulting from, incident response activities.

*The hunt team initiates a hunt anytime an IOC or other intelligence regarding threat activities are received from recognized intelligence (CTI) or support activity. The hunt team will __always__ initiate a hunt at the direction of the IR function.*

The following evaluation criteria are used by the hunt team to determine if a hunt should be initiated, or if further evaluation of a hunt request is required:

| IOC Criteria | Factors that Support Hunt Initiation |
|---|---|
| Source | • Source has a history of providing high-confidence indicators. |
| Ease of Search | • The capability exists to search for the specific type and format of IOC. |
| Relevance | • The IOC is associated with malicious activity targeting industry peers or other relevant groups.<br>• The IOC is related to technologies, applications, systems, etc., that are currently deployed. |
| Exposure | • The IOC is associated with malicious activity exploiting known vulnerabilities that exist within the IT environment.<br>• The infection vector of the associated malicious activity is related and relevant to the regular activities or its users (e.g., watering hole attacks on a popular public websites). |
| Existing Coverage | • Existing deployed security solutions are confirmed, or unlikely, to have detection rules for the IOC. |
| Impact | • The IOC is associated with high-impact activity that may cause significant compromise to information or systems (e.g., Advance Persistent Threats[6] (APT), hacktivism, remote access tools, credential harvesters, etc.) |

---

[6] APTs are typically nation-state cyber-activities supported by a nation. The top 3 major countries are China, Russia, and Iran, that specifically target US federal agencies and companies.

| 1.3 | | Determine Search Timelines |
|---|---|---|

| Input | | Initiation of a new hunt |
|---|---|---|
| **RACI** | **R** IR Team Lead | Responsible for analyzing the IOC and available supporting information to determine the appropriate search timeline. IR Team will determine the approximate amount of time and resources to ensure proper coverage of the hunt activity. |
| | **A** Hunt Team Lead | Accountable to ensure that the hunt timeline is appropriately scoped, monitored, and met. |
| | **C** Trigger Source(s) | Consulted to provide input on the hunt timeline. |
| | **I** Trigger Source(s) | Informed of the next stage of analysis. |

**Details**

The IR team determines the search timeline for the hunt based on the following criteria for each respective input source:

**Cyber Threat Intelligence**

*Watchlist*

The search timeline for an IOC originating from a threat intelligence feed should align with the recommendation issued by the IOC source. A default of a ninety (90) days should be used if no recommended search timeline has been suggested by the IOC source.

*IOC - Recommendation to Hunt*

The search timeline for an IOC with a recommendation to hunt from the CTI function should be determined by the CTI function and included with the hunt request.

*IOC –Recommendation to Hunt Has Not Been Included*

A default of a ninety (90) days should be used for an IOC originating from the CTI function with no recommendation to hunt included.

**Business Case Development**

A default of a ninety (90) days should be used for an IOC originating from the case development function.

**Incident Response**

The search timeline for an IOC from the IR function should be determined by the IR function and included with the hunt request.

| | |
|---|---|
| **Output** | Hunt request search timelines established. |

| 1.4 | | | Hunt Based upon IOC Type |
|---|---|---|---|
| **Input** | | Hunt request with established search timeline | |
| **RACI** | R | Hunt Team Analyst | Responsible for performing the hunt. |
| | A | Hunt Team Lead | Accountable to ensure that the hunt is appropriately performed. |
| | C | Hunt Team | Consulted regarding the hunt methodology as required. |
| | I | Hunt Team | Informed of the hunt details to ensure coordination. |
| **Details** | | The hunt team analysts perform the hunt based on the established search timelines and IOC type and follows the analyst procedures. | |
| | | The following guidance is used to perform the hunt for each respective IOC type (all historical searches are to be limited to the established search | |

timelines). If an analyst directs access a security device is not feasible, interrogation of SIEM or a centralized log management system may be leveraged for hunting purposes.

# Hunt Guidance

| IOC Type | |
|---|---|
| **Email** | Perform a search using the email security solution where the specific indicator (e.g., subject, sender, message body, etc.) matches the IOC. |
| **File** | Create a new indicator on, for example, FireEye HX® with one or more of the following file conditions (as applicable/available) that match the IOC:<br><br>a. File path: *equal, contains,* or *matches*<br>b. SHA-256[7]: *equal*<br>c. File size (in bytes): *equal* |
| **IP Address** | 1. Perform a search for:<br><br>a. Successful or denied firewall connections where the source or destination Internet Protocol (IP) address matches the IOC.<br><br>b. Successful or denied web proxy events where the source or destination IP address matches the IOC.<br><br>c. Intrusion Detection System (IDS)/Intrusion Prevention System (IPS) events where the source or destination IP address matches the IOC.<br><br>d. Successful or denied web application firewall events where the source or destination IP address matches the IOC.<br><br>2. Create a new indicator with one or more of the following Network Connection conditions (as applicable/available) that match the IOC:<br>a. Local or remote (destination) IP addresses: *equal*<br>b. Local or remote (destination) ports: *equal, is greater than, is less than,* and *is between.* |

---

[7] SHA-256 is the federally recommended hashing standard. Older versions, such as MD-5 is highly-breakable and is no longer in use by most major corporations due to its current vulnerabilities.

| | |
|---|---|
| **Network (string, traffic pattern, user agent)** | 1. Review externally-facing, perimeter, and internal IDS logs (as applicable) where the specific network artifact indicator matches the IOC.<br><br>2. Perform a search of web and application logs on vulnerable externally-facing systems where the specific network artifact indicator matches the IOC.<br><br>3. Perform a search on any existing Web Application Firewalls (WAF) on vulnerable externally-facing systems where the specific network artifact indicator matches the IOC. |
| **Registry Key** | Create a new indicator in, for example, FireEye HX® that matches the IOC. |
| **URL** | 1. Perform a search for web proxy events where the Uniform Resource Locator (URL) matches the IOC.<br><br>2. Create a new indicator with the following Domain Name Service (DNS) Lookup condition that matches the IOC:<br>   a. DNS lookup: *equal, contains,* or *matches* |
| **SIEM** | In lieu of analysts having direct access to the security devices, interrogation of SIEM or centralized log management system will be leveraged for hunt. |
| **Output** | ***Completed hunt*** |

| 1.5 | | | Outcome |
|------|---|------|---------|
| **Input** | | | Completed hunt |
| **RACI** | R | Hunt Team Analyst | Responsible for ensuring that any required referral occurs depending on the hunt outcome. |
| | A | Hunt Team Lead | Accountable to ensure that any required referral occurs depending on the hunt outcome. |
| | C | Trigger Source(s) | Consulted regarding the hunt outcome prior to referral or hunt process completion. |
| | I | Trigger Source(s) | Informed of the hunt outcome |
| **Details** | | | The hunt concludes with one of the following three outcomes: |

**Something Discovered: Malicious**

An active or historic compromise which may currently or have previously placed its assets, or its **data**[8] at risk; Discovered during the hunt activity.

**Something Discovered: Non-Malicious**

Violation(s) of acceptable use or organizational policies discovered during the hunt.

**Nothing Discovered**

No indication of active compromise or behavior violating acceptable use or organizational policies discovered.

| **Output** | | | Completed hunt. |
|------|---|------|---------|

---

[8] **Data** is the main item within any network that should be specifically protected especially if is of a sensitive or restricted nature; modern-day cybersecurity protections are focused on data protection.

| 1.6 | | | Refer to Incident Response |
|------|---|---|---------------------------|
| **Input** | | | Completed hunt with malicious finding. |
| **RACI** | R | Hunt Team Analyst | Responsible for ensuring that all required information and context is referred to the appropriate IR function. |
| | A | Hunt Team Lead | Accountable for ensuring that all required information and context is referred to the IR function. |
| | C | Incident Response Team | Consulted regarding referral process. |
| | I | Incident Response Team | Informed of the malicious finding. |
| **Details** | | | All information regarding the hunt and the details of the malicious finding is compiled by the hunt team analyst and referred to the IR function. |
| **Output** | | | Referral to the affected IR function. |

| 1.7 | | | Raise as a Potential Compliance Issue[9] |
|------|---|---|------------------------------------------|
| **Input** | | | Completed hunt with non-malicious finding |
| **RACI** | R | Hunt Team Analyst | Responsible for ensuring that all required information and context is handed to the relevant internal function(s) for escalation as a *compliance issue*. |
| | A | Hunt Team Lead | Accountable for ensuring that all required information and context is handed to the relevant internal function(s) for escalation as a compliance issue. |

---

[9] Some businesses and agencies identify "best practice" violations as a compliance issue. *It is not.* Failures of best practice may include, for example, weak passwords or leaving smart cards unattended. Such failures must be captured and enforceable through acceptable use or like business policies are Human Resource sanctioned policies and laws for the punishment of an individual.

| | | |
|---|---|---|
| C | Relevant Internal Function(s) | Consulted regarding referral process. |
| I | Relevant Internal Function(s) | Informed of the non-malicious finding. |

| | |
|---|---|
| Details | All information regarding the hunt and the details of the non-malicious finding is compiled by the hunt team analyst [CyA] and referred to the relevant internal function(s) to include senior leadership for escalation as a compliance issue. |
| Output | Refer to the relevant internal function(s). |

| 1.8 | | | Update MHTDB |
|---|---|---|---|
| **Input** | | Completed hunt. | |
| **RACI** | R | Hunt Team Analyst | Responsible for ensuring the MHTDB is updated with all required information regarding the completed hunt and outcome. |
| | A | Hunt Team Lead | Accountable for ensuring the MHTDB is updated with all required information regarding the completed hunt and outcome. |
| | C | N/A | N/A |
| | I | Hunt Team Trigger Source(s) | Informed of the completed hunt and outcome. |
| **Details** | | The hunt team analyst updates the MHTDB with all required information regarding the completed hunt and outcome and notifies | |

| | the trigger source(s) that the hunt has been completed and provides the results. |
|---|---|
| **Output** | Completed hunt process |

### Base Hunting (Internally-focused)

Base hunting is used typically to monitor compliance and "insider threat" activities. It can be initiated based upon known or suspected activities from within the agency or may be used to conduct ad hoc inspection of individuals and sub-agencies that may be in non-compliance with corporate or agency acceptable use policies and procedures.

The following flowchart shows the detailed flow of the *base* hunt workflow.

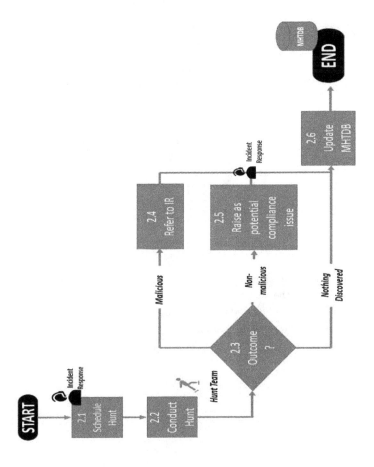

*Graphic 5. Hunt Request (Internally focused)*

**Base Hunting - RACI Matrix**

| 2.1 | | | Schedule Hunt |
|---|---|---|---|
| **Input** | | | Base hunt triggered by "hunt schedule[10]" |
| **RACI** | **R** | Hunt Team | Responsible for maintaining an awareness of the hunt schedule and performing time management accordingly. |
| | **A** | Hunt Team Lead | Accountable to ensure that the hunt schedule is being adhered to and that the required resources are appropriately managed. |
| | **C** | N/A | N/A |
| | **I** | N/A | N/A |
| **Details** | | | The base hunt schedule specifies the frequency that the base hunt is to be performed. The next hunt run-date and time are recorded in the MTHDB. Upcoming base hunts will be added to the queue and assigned to an available hunt team member. |
| **Output** | | | Base hunt queued for action. |

---

[10] A "hunt schedule" is usually an ad hoc inspection of the agency's IT environment that is coordinated between IR and Hunt personnel. It is typically restricted to personnel with a need-to-only purpose.

| 2.2 | | Conduct Hunt | |
|------|---|---|---|
| **Input** | | Base hunt queued to be performed. | |
| **RACI** | **R** | Hunt Team Analyst | Responsible for performing the hunt. |
| | **A** | Hunt Team Lead | Accountable to ensure that the hunt is appropriately performed. |
| | **C** | Hunt Team | Consulted regarding the hunt methodology as required. |
| | **I** | Hunt Team | Informed of the hunt details to ensure coordination. |
| **Details** | | The hunt team analyst performs the hunt based on the hunt activities and established search timelines as established in the MTHDB. | |
| **Output** | | Hunt completed. | |

| 2.3 | | Outcome | |
|------|---|---|---|
| **Input** | | Hunt completed | |
| **RACI** | **R** | Hunt Team Analyst | Responsible for ensuring that any required referral occurs depending on the final hunt outcome. |
| | **A** | Hunt Team Lead | Accountable to ensure that any required referral occurs depending on the final hunt outcome. |
| | **C** | N/A | N/A |
| | **I** | N/A | N/A |

| Details | The hunt concludes with one of the following three outcomes:

**Something Discovered: Malicious**

Active or historic compromise, which may currently or have previously placed, its assets, or its information at risk, discovered during the hunt.

**Something Discovered: Non-Malicious**

Violation(s) of acceptable use or organizational policies discovered during the hunt.

**Nothing Discovered**

No indication of active compromise or behavior violating acceptable use or organizational policies. |
|---|---|
| Output | Completed hunt |

| 2.4 | | Refer to Incident Response | |
|---|---|---|---|
| Input | | Completed hunt with malicious finding | |
| RACI | R | Hunt Team Analyst | Responsible for ensuring that all required information and context is handed to the appropriate IR function. |
| | A | Hunt Team Lead | Accountable for ensuring that all required information and context is handed to the appropriate IR function. |
| | C | Incident Response Team | Consulted regarding referral process. |

| | | Incident Response Team | Informed of malicious findings |
|---|---|---|---|
| **Details** | | All information regarding the hunt and the details of the malicious finding is compiled by the hunt team analyst and provided to the affected IR function. | |
| **Output** | | Refer to the IR function. | |

| 2.5 | | | Raise a Potential Compliance Issue |
|---|---|---|---|
| **Input** | | | Completed hunt with non-malicious finding. |
| **RACI** | R | Hunt Team Analyst | Responsible for ensuring that all required information and context is provided to the relevant internal function(s)[11] for escalation as a compliance issue. |
| | A | Hunt Team Lead | Accountable for ensuring that all required information and context is given to the relevant internal function(s) for escalation as a compliance issue. |
| | C | Relevant Internal Function(s) | Consulted regarding referred to process. |
| | I | Relevant Internal Function(s) | Informed of the non-malicious finding. |
| **Details** | | | All information regarding the hunt and the details of the non-malicious finding is compiled by the hunt team analyst and provided to the relevant internal function(s) for escalation as a compliance issue. |
| **Output** | | | Handoff to relevant internal function(s) |

---

[11] This could include senior leadership, an individual's direct supervisor, or Human Resources (HR) to begin disciplinary actions and documentation requirements.

| 2.6 | | Update MHTDB | |
|------|---|---|---|
| **Input** | | Completed hunt | |
| **RACI** | **R** | Hunting Team Analyst | Responsible for ensuring the MHTDB is updated with all required information regarding the completed hunt and outcome. |
| | **A** | Hunting Team Lead | Accountable for ensuring the MHTDB is updated with all required information regarding the completed hunt and outcome. |
| | **C** | N/A | N/A |
| | **I** | Hunting Team | Informed of the completed hunt and outcome. |
| **Details** | | The hunting team analyst updates the MHTDB with all required information regarding the completed hunt and outcome. | |
| **Output** | | Completed hunt process | |

# Metrics

A Hunt program should provide weekly, monthly, and annual metrics to corporate or agency leadership. The weekly metrics provide information regarding threats reviewed during the past week and any anticipated activities based upon sound analytical tradecraft and IOCs seen active within the infrastructure. (Also, see Appendix C, *Can the Human Poet Bring Value to Predictive Analysis?* This is a discussion on how human experts can work with growing data analytic science capabilities, and the value to cybersecurity analysis in the near-future.)

The monthly metrics report should provide trends and resource utilization. Trends should be tied to common malicious intrusions and external intelligence sources that are cooperative with a part of the critical infrastructure. Annual metrics provides a holistic view of the Hunting program to ensure it meets business objectives, additional resourcing needed, and cooperative information sharing activities within the critical infrastructure for which an agency belongs.

### Weekly Metrics

Weekly metrics reporting for the Hunting program will occur in a weekly status report. Weekly metrics include the outcomes of hunts completed during the prior seven days. Metrics should include IOCs identified and resolved during the prior week. It should also include final analytic reports created and disseminated to both internal divisions and external partners to include the federal government.

### Monthly Metrics

Monthly metrics for the hunting program will be reported and delivered during the first full week of each calendar month. The monthly metrics report will provide metrics regarding hunting program functions, including:

- Hunts conducted by attack lifecycle
- Hunt outcomes
- Hunts transferred to business case development
- Hunts escalated to the Incident Response team

### Annual Metrics

Annual metrics will provide a view of where the hunting program has improved over the year and aligned with the companies or agencies strategic goals. It should also present any issues faced by the hunt program such as a lack of necessary tools or data sources to complete effective hunt operations.

### Qualitative versus Quantitative Metrics

The best metrics are those that can:

1. **Be measurable or quantified, and**
2. **Provide value to the agency**

There are several measures that can be used, however, we do not recommend the Risk Matrix approach. (See next section regarding *The Fallacy of The Risk Reporting Matrix).* The risk matrix introduces too many unsubstantiated unknowns and should be deferred to more meaningful metrics built from within the business's operational needs and necessities.

Metrics should be derived by the value created by CTI and Hunt personnel responding (time factor) and effectively (intrusion caught and minimized) mitigating threats to the IT environment. No metrics are ever a certainty for security but provides needed insight to managerial oversight needed not just within the area of cybersecurity protection and response.

---

### The Fallacy of The Risk Reporting Matrix

The Risk Reporting Matrix (RRM) is a classic means to characterize the levels of risk (Under Secretary of Defense for Acquisition, Technology, and Logistics, 2006) to programs and initiatives to include the risks to the defense department, program management efforts, and the cybersecurity community. Its representation is simplistic, but its implications are far-reaching. Hayden (2010) and Hubbard and Seiersen (2016) have major issues with current methodologies used to assess risk across industries, but cybersecurity specifically. "They are a failure. They do not work" (Hubbard & Seiersen, 2016, p. 14); the RRM is one of their specific concerns.

The RRM requires users to apply subjective labels to a typical 5x5 matrix; Figure 1 provides an example of an RRM (University of Melbourne, 2018) where the "likelihood" or probability is on the vertical and "consequence" or impact are across the horizontal axes. Users are to: "[d]evelop *probability* [emphasis added] and consequence scales by allocating thresholds across the WBS [Work Breakdown Structure]..." (Under Secretary of Defense for Acquisition, Technology, and Logistics, 2006, p. 14), but they are not provided the back-end methodologies or mathematics to derive such calculations. The RRM was never designed or defined to be a quantitative risk measure (Project Management Skills, 2010). Practitioners of Risk Management (RM) and the recipients of RRM reporting have assumed it is founded upon solid analyses and statistics; they have unfortunately been wrong.

| Likelihood | Consequence | | | | |
|---|---|---|---|---|---|
| | Insignificant | Minor | Moderate | Major | Severe |
| Almost certain | Medium | High | High | Extreme | Extreme |
| Likely | Medium | Medium | High | Extreme | Extreme |
| Possible | Low | Medium | Medium | High | Extreme |
| Unlikely | Low | Low | Medium | High | High |
| Rare | Low | Low | Low | Medium | High |

*Figure 1.* Health & safety – Risk matrix and definitions. Adapted from "Risk Assessment Methodology" by the University of Melbourne, p. 11, Copyright 2018 by the University of Melbourne.

While there is seldom one solution to any problem, the initial solution is the elimination of the RRM. While its abandonment is basic in nature, it would remove the interpretation that it is based upon objective mathematical precision by users that the RRM is ideal in the identification and management of risk. "Our somewhat naïve definition of risk in the context of IT security is mirrored by the lack of rigor we tend to demonstrate in measuring it" (Hayden, 2010, p. 9). The elimination of the RRM is the first step to improving our ability to better assess cybersecurity risk because it gives a false sense of assessing risk.

Hubbard and Seiersen (2016) provide one significantly accepted commercial approach. They introduce the initial foundation of establishing a "quantitative risk assessment" (Hubbard & Seiersen, 2016, p. 35) process. This method relies on the *subjective* expertise of individuals within the field of cybersecurity and leads to an *objective* mathematical output. They begin with replacing the subjective RRM terms, as the metrics of "high," "medium," and "low." They replace them with new probabilities and dollar impacts based upon expert knowledge. They present a modern means to include expert knowledge and experience to formulate an improved solution.

This answer portends an ongoing refinement and provides the framework to progress predictive analytics needed to improve the field of cybersecurity RM. Hubbard and Seiersen's (2016) process identifies the anticipated risks by the Subject Matter Expert (SME) who define over a period that the risk may in fact occur. This process includes assigning subjective probability scoring of 0-100% that will become part of the SME's overall prediction. The next step is to assign an actual range of monetary cost if the event were to occur within a 90% Confidence Interval (CI); this bounds the estimate within a range of a 90% probability whether a risk occurs, and an estimate of a business cost range is additionally included (Hubbard & Seiersen, 2016).

The final step is the total of all expert predictions are averaged and become the foundation of both a final probability (e.g. a 65% likelihood) and uncertainty (i.e. within the established 90% CI of this methodology) process refinement (Hubbard & Seiersen, 2016). This becomes the key basis of better risk predictions as historically found in the experiment by Sir Francis Galton in 1906. In this experiment, Galton took a collection of individual "expert" predictions and averaged them to forecast the actual weight of a slaughtered cow by within one pound of its actual weight (Tetlock & Gardner, 2016).

These combined solutions are substantive and optimal to the progress of improving the state of cybersecurity RM. It would move the state of predictive cybersecurity RM to better than a dart throwing chimpanzee (Tetlock & Gardner, 2016). It would remove the RRM that introduces a damaging flaw in the mental belief that it represents quantified certainty. Hubbard and Seiersen (2016) introduced the next critical step—to instead use the of experts focused on better confined and probabilistic evaluations and predictions. The subjective expertise of individuals thus "bridges" us closer to a more objective means to assess and predict risk.

There are other solutions that are more heavily mathematically based such as the use of Monte Carlo and regression models. These lend themselves to more objective outcomes; however, they do not leverage the accumulation of knowledge of SMEs. Mathematical models may be better, but are devoid of human knowledge, experience, and intuition that can identify the elements of uncertainty and surprise that are more difficult to introduce into a mathematical algorithm. While none of this reduces cost, time, or convenience, they do supplement our ability to better predict the consequences of risk to the user, agency, or company.

There is seldom a singular best solution. There are more typically optimal solutions. The more answers introduced to mitigate a problem, the greater the chance of success in solving the overall problem. The elimination of the RRM is necessitated not because it is a bad model, but because its presence introduces a false sense of security and certainty. Unless actual mathematical rigor is implemented by its use, it must be retired immediately.

Finally, Hubbard and Seiersen's (2016) work is an important beginning to bringing predictive analysis aligned more with accepted mathematical norms. This includes the ability of SMEs to attain an objective outcome. It would advance cybersecurity RM and eliminate the lack of real objectivity hidden behind a false and historical acceptance of the flawed RRM.

# References for "The Fallacy of The Risk Reporting Matrix"

Hayden, L. (2010). *IT security metrics: A practical framework for measuring security & protecting data.* New York: McGraw Hill.

Hubbard, D., & Seiersen, R. (2016). *How to measure anything in cybersecurity risk.* Hoboken, NJ: John wiley & sons.

Project Management Skills. (2010, September 5). *Qualitative risk analysis and assessment.* Retrieved from Project Management Skills: https://www.project-management-skills.com/qualitative-risk-analysis.html

Tetlock, P., & Gardner, D. (2016). *Superforecasting: The art and science of prediction.* New York: Random House.

Under Secretary of Defense for Acquisition, Technology, and Logistics. (2006, August). *Risk management guide for DOD acquisition.* Retrieved from Office of the Under Secretary of Defense for Acquisition, Technology, and Logistics: https://www.acq.osd.mil/damir/documents/DAES_2006_RISK_GUIDE.pdf

Under Secretary of Defense for Acquisition, Technology, and Logistics. (2017, January). *Risk, issue, and opportunity management guide for defense acquisition programs.* Retrieved from Office of the Under Secretary of Defense for Acquisition, Technology, and Logistics: https://www.acq.osd.mil/se/docs/2017-rio.pdf

University of Melbourne. (2018, May). *Risk assessment methodology.* Retrieved from University of Melbourne: https://safety.unimelb.edu.au/__data/assets/pdf_file/0007/1716712/health-and-safety-risk-assessment-methodology.pdf

# PART II - Tactical Activities of the Threat Hunt Process

## The THP Tactical Methodology

The following pages provide a detailed depiction of the procedures for a "Hunt Mission Program," centered on the four areas specific areas that modestly parallels the Intelligence Community's Intelligence Lifecycle. Both the CTI Analysts and Hunt Team analysts will work cooperatively throughout the THP Methodology. IR personnel may also play a role and will act as approval of any current or continued action against any known or suspected occurrence.

An effective Hunt Mission Program relies upon the following four areas:

1. **Designate**
2. **Acquire**
3. **Analyze**
4. **Reporting**

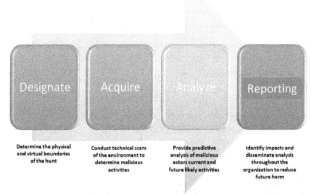

| Designate | Acquire | Analyze | Reporting |
| --- | --- | --- | --- |
| Determine the physical and virtual boundaries of the hunt | Conduct technical scans of the environment to determine malicious activities | Provide predictive analysis of malicious actors current and future likely activities | Identify impacts and disseminate analysis throughout the organization to reduce future harm |

*Graphic 6. The THP Tactical Methodology*

The THP Methodology begins with defining the boundaries that need to be identified as part of hunt activities. *Designate* identifies all IT hardware, software, network assets, etc., that likely are directly affected by known or suspected malicious activities. Without a clear understanding of boundaries, analytic resources may be inadvertently diverted or distracted by not defining the scope of the effort.

*Acquire* is identical to the collection phase of the Intelligence Lifecycle. In this phase CTI analysts conduct technical scans of the targeted IT environment to determine malicious activities. Varied scans are used to detect unauthorized port access, identify types of injected malware, use IOC databases to determine potential threats, etc. Acquire gathers all relevant data and facts around an event or incident for the purposes of organizational action and IR alerts to senior and government officials as required by policy or law.

In the *Analyze* phase, Hunt team members, in close coordination with CTI personnel, determine the who, what, where, etc., factors in order to identify attribution of the attack and whether the attack rises to the level of a reportable event or incident. Analyze is a continual process that develops intelligence reports and offers predictive intelligence to the organization and third-party cooperative businesses or agency members. Analyze provides critical (immediate), short-term (within 24 hours), and long-term (typically monthly) analytical reports to members of both the technical and non-technical personnel of the organization; this phase is identical within the Intelligence Lifecycle.

Finally, **Reporting** identifies impacts to the IT environment, and supports resourcing identification and demands where senior leaders must play a decisive role. Reporting also ensures the quality review of reporting and ensures its timely dissemination throughout the organization. Senior leaders are accountable to ensuring critical intelligence identification and communications are timely to reduce especially malicious activities against the company or agency's infrastructure.

The following sections provide greater "tactical" clarity for members of the Hunt Team, CTI Analysts, IR personnel, and Senior Leaders. This more descriptive application of the Hunt teams' efforts begins with *Designate*.

---

## 1. Designate:

The focus of the *Designate* phase is to develop a hypothesis. Formulate a Hypothesis or hypotheses, as appropriate. The hypothesis can be based on several different inputs including:

- Internal use business scenarios
- Threat exposure checks (Base Hunts)[12]
- Incident response activities
- CTI

The hypothesis should consider:

- **Source confidence** – the source has a history of proving high-confidence indicators.
- **Expected ease of the search** – the capability exists to search for

[12] A **base hunt**, or **threat exposure check**, is defined as a repeatable search based on analytical methodology which produces a low fidelity results (i.e., results that require analyst review and cannot be fully automated as a rule); these hunts will reside in the MHTDB.

the specific type, indicators, and format of the IOC.

- **Target and searchable data of relevance** – The IOC is associated with malicious activity targeting, industry peers or other relevant groups. Also, the IOC may be related to technologies, applications, etc., that are currently deployed within the IT environment.
- **Known exposure** – The IOC is associated with malicious activity exploiting known vulnerabilities that exist in the environment. The IOC is also used to identify the attack vector of the malicious activity, and a determination whether it is related and relevant to normal operational activities.
- **Existing infrastructure and visibility** – Existing tools are confirmed to have visibility or detection capability for the specific IOC.
- **Potential impact** – The IOC is associated with high-impact activity that may cause significant damage in the event of a compromise.

The hypothesis should also answer a basic set of standard questions that help scope and define the hunt.

- What are we looking for?
- Where will we look?
- What do we expect to find or not find?
- Why are we looking for it?
- What will its presence or absence tell us?
- Who or what will consume the outputs?

After developing the hypothesis, the analyst will next:

- Identify the target criteria
- Establish a timeframe and expected duration of the hunt in coordination with IR personnel.
- Identify execution resources and constraints
- Establish expected outcomes
- Communicate intent and scope to leadership and stakeholders

**Metrics**: The data fields that may provide value to technical and non-technical leadership may include:

- Case records
- Dates opened
- Expected start and end times
- Actual start time and end times
- Hypotheses

- Objective summaries
- Target criteria and supporting information
- Source or use case
- Stakeholder output
- Target IOCs

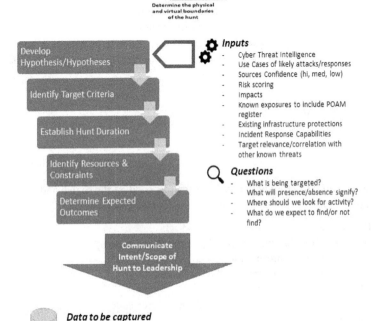

**Designate**

Determine the physical
and virtual boundaries
of the hunt

Develop
Hypothesis/Hypotheses

Identify Target Criteria

Establish Hunt Duration

Identify Resources &
Constraints

Determine Expected
Outcomes

Communicate
Intent/Scope of
Hunt to Leadership

**Inputs**
- Cyber Threat Intelligence
- Use Cases of likely attacks/responses
- Sources Confidence (hi, med, low)
- Risk scoring
- Impacts
- Known exposures to include POAM register
- Existing infrastructure protections
- Incident Response Capabilities
- Target relevance/correlation with other known threats

**Questions**
- What is being targeted?
- What will presence/absence signify?
- Where should we look for activity?
- What do we expect to find/or not find?

**Data to be captured**
- Case Record
- Hypothesis/hypotheses
- Date opened
- Source or Use case
- Objective summary
- Start/stop date/time
- Target found/forensics (IP addresses, MAC, etc.)
- Indicators of Compromise (IOC) correlation (correct, not correct, or new)

Figure 1. **'Designate' Workflow and Considerations**

## 2. **Acquire:**

The next area of the hunt process is the Acquire phase. This may also be referred to as the collection phase. The CyA will access tools and data to begin the collection of vital data for the purposes of determining the level of intrusion and associated risks to the company or agency.

**Access Tools and Data** – Primary candidate tools may include, for example, Splunk®, FireEye HX®, the FireEye PX Tech-Enabler®, and other internal information and toolsets. This effort does not necessarily flow from internal tools; however, it should provide adequate support for forensic artifacts or other data log collections.

The analysts will **Aggregate and Prepare Target Data**, to include IOCs, and determine the whether the data is relevant or of interest. The analysts will primarily, but not exclusively, use this information to formulate:

- Specific IOCs
- CTI extracts and references
- Incident response data
- Previous hunt mission data
- Environmental knowledge

**Search infrastructure and data** – the analysts conduct the search and depending on the type of IOCs. The search will collect the following types of data:

- Domain names
- Hypertext Transfer Protocol (HTTP) methods and code
- Endpoint registry information
- Simple Mail Transfer Protocol (SMTP) Header data
- File names, paths and types
- Hypertext Markup Language (HTML)/Java source code
- File sizes
- Uniform Resource Identifier (URI) strings
- Uniform Resource Locators (URL)
- Process names
- Source and destination ports and protocols
- File hashes
- Destination Internet Protocols (IP)
- Attachment names and hashes
- Byte counts (transferred)
- User-agent strings
- Attacker/Source IPs

**Validate Completion of Searches** – the *Hunt analyst will validate the data* from the searches and answer the following:

- Is the target data searchable by the tools and the infrastructure?
- Did all searches from all sources complete as expected?
- Were searches completed within an acceptable timeframe?
- Were there any undesirable or unexpected results?
- Was there any outlier[13] ("black swan") concerns raised by the search? Should it be further monitored/reported?

**Initial analysis** is performed in a triage manner to determine if immediate or high impact threats were detected, and if so, those are escalated using the established IR Plan (IRP). The IR staff will be notified. If there are no findings, the analyst then **Documents the Findings and Updates the Case Status**. This will include updates to the MHTDB in order to support ongoing trend analysis efforts. It is important that even events become part of the MHTDB record because while the event may have been determined to be reportable it may be a precursor of a future attack.[14]

**Metrics:** The data fields for compiling suggested potential metrics include:

- Initial analysis
- Actual correlated target data
- Infrastructure searched
- High fidelity indicators
- Summary of search result success and failures
- Escalation to the IR function

---

[13] An outlier or "black swan" event in a low or unexpected occurrence based on past historical data and intelligence. While these are uncommon, they may highlight new and changing Tactics, Techniques and Procedures (TTP) by hackers.

[14] Nation-states hackers may conduct low-level "probing" actions to identify weaknesses in corporate perimeters and networks. They are intended to ascertain the level of defensive complexity an environment may or may not have to future attack.

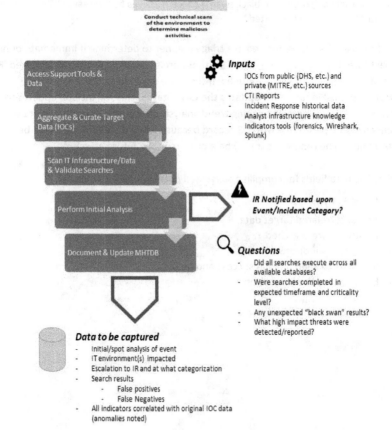

**Acquire**

Conduct technical scans of the environment to determine malicious activities

Access Support Tools & Data

Aggregate & Curate Target Data (IOCs)

Scan IT Infrastructure/Data & Validate Searches

Perform Initial Analysis

Document & Update MHTDB

**Inputs**
- IOCs from public (DHS, etc.) and private (MITRE, etc.) sources
- CTI Reports
- Incident Response historical data
- Analyst infrastructure knowledge
- Indicators tools (forensics, Wireshark, Splunk)

*IR Notified based upon Event/Incident Category?*

**Questions**
- Did all searches execute across all available databases?
- Were searches completed in expected timeframe and criticality level?
- Any unexpected "black swan" results?
- What high impact threats were detected/reported?

**Data to be captured**
- Initial/spot analysis of event
- IT environment(s) impacted
- Escalation to IR and at what categorization
- Search results
    - False positives
    - False Negatives
- All indicators correlated with original IOC data (anomalies noted)

**Figure 2. 'Acquire' Workflow and Considerations**

## 3. Analyze

Once the search has completed, the analysts will begin the Analyze phase. The basic analysis tasks consist of:

- Modify and re-execute searches, if needed
  - Determine level of risk to the IT environment
  - Determine attribution of the attacker by IP address, etc.
  - Validate target matches
  - Correlate contextual intelligence
  - Modify target searches
  - New target activity
  - Sort data set
  - Formulate analytic products

- Sort, links and prioritize data events and threat activity
- Identify additional indicators (IOC) and target activity
- If necessary, initiate a new hunt based on a newly discovered data. Is the threat based on modified target activity or new specific IOCs?

**Inferential analysis** – will be performed based on the analyst's knowledge of the environment, the operational exposure, and business intelligence factors. Questions that should be asked may include:

- What determination can be made based on the facts and empirical data?
- How has the original hunt hypothesis been proven or disproven?
- What key data do we know and what do we not know?

The remaining tasks during the Analyze phase are to determine infrastructure **attack vectors** and related **Tactics, Techniques, and Procedures (TTPs)**. Analysis **correlated** CTI may assist in determining threat sources, actor motivations, and capabilities.

**Determine effectiveness** of existing security controls, and if needed, suggest improvements or new security controls.

**Metrics:** The suggested data fields for compiling metrics are:

- Malicious findings
- Non-malicious findings
- Analytic determinations
- Malware variants identified
- Common IOCs or patterns

- Total IOCs detected
- Vulnerabilities exploited
- Affected/targeted business units
- Intelligence summary data (key points)
- Security control failures and success
- Affected infrastructure
- Affected geographic locations
- Threat actor attribution
- Chronology of exposure

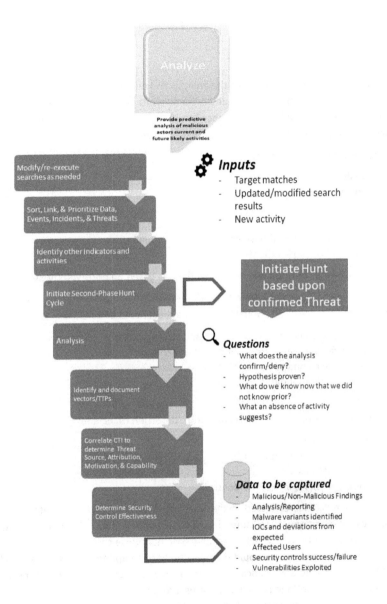

**Analyze**

Provide predictive
analysis of malicious
actors current and
future likely activities

Modify/re-execute
searches as needed

Sort, Link, & Prioritize Data,
Events, Incidents, & Threats

Identify other indicators and
activities

Initiate Second-Phase Hunt
Cycle

Analysis

Identify and document
vectors/TTPs

Correlate CTI to
determine Threat
Source, Attribution,
Motivation, & Capability

Determine Security
Control Effectiveness

**Inputs**
- Target matches
- Updated/modified search results
- New activity

Initiate Hunt
based upon
confirmed Threat

**Questions**
- What does the analysis confirm/deny?
- Hypothesis proven?
- What do we know now that we did not know prior?
- What an absence of activity suggests?

**Data to be captured**
- Malicious/Non-Malicious Findings
- Analysis/Reporting
- Malware variants identified
- IOCs and deviations from expected
- Affected Users
- Security controls success/failure
- Vulnerabilities Exploited

Figure 3. 'Analyze' Workflow and Considerations

## 4. Reporting

The Reporting phase finalizes the analysis and distributes the reporting. Feedback in this phase is essential for continued process improvement. Determine the overall **business impact** (functional and financial) considering the knowledge of the environment, the organizational exposure, and current business intelligence.

Develop a **threat summary**.

- Analytical determinations
- Affected users
- Security control failures/successes
- Geographic locations affected
- Affected or targeted business units or individuals
- Intelligence requirements

Form **strategic outlook** and recommendations based on observed threats.

**Identify gaps in strategic (and tactical) intelligence** and collections. Formulate new intelligence requirements. General questions that should be asked are:

- What CTI are we missing tactically and strategically?
- What can we automate to limit further exposure?
- How do we communicate this to stakeholders?
- What recommendations do we make?
- Can we improve the process?

**Identify data** for blocks and alerts for future detection to include:

- CTI portal data
- CTI process elements
- SIEM watch lists
- Blocks or alerts in security controls

The intelligence collected in the hunt can now be analyzed to determine if **new business cases or new base hunts** should be developed. If so, this should be referenced in hunt documentation as well as the new base hunts/use cases.

The new intelligence should now also be used to **update the intelligence lifecycle** with new strategic and tactical CTI. Intelligence is rarely an end-to-end process and operates as a continuous cycle. Updates are part of the continuous improvement process necessary to improve all phases of the process.

The analyst next identifies scenarios and indicators to **mitigate future exposure**. While not possible in every case, this topic should be discussed with security engineers, cybersecurity professionals, consultants, and Subject Matter Experts (SME) in order to explore ways to further mitigate future risk to the environment.

Finally, the analyst will **distribute and deliver intelligence reporting** and gain feedback for process improvement. This will typically result in analytic notes and database updates to the MHTDB, and where a more extensive incident has occurred will *require* a formal After-Action Report (AAR) event; AARs are the foundation of effective continual improvement efforts and processes.

**Metrics:** The following data fields are recommended as candidate metrics for measuring effectiveness of overall THP:

- Realized organizational impact
- Full threat report or threat summary
- Archive of all data collected during the trend analysis
- Report distribution tracking
- New intelligence requirements based on the completed hunt

- After action items (internal and business units)
- Intelligence gaps
- Process or collection gaps
- Stakeholder Requests for Information/Intelligence (RFI) and Product Requests for Changes (RFC)

**Inputs**
- Analysis/Tradecraft
- Security Controls' Postures
- Affected Organizations
- Business Intelligence (Overall Risks)

**Questions**
- What CTI is missing tactically/strategically?
- How to better automate detection/exposure?
- What recommendations should be made to IR and Sr. Leadership?
- How can we improve the process?

**Data to be captured**
- Impacts
- Threat Reporting
- Document archiving
- Document retention
- After Action Report (continual improvement)
- Intelligence Gaps

Reporting

Identify impacts and disseminate analysis throughout the organization to reduce future harm

Overall Business Impact

Develop Threat Summary & Intelligence Reports

Form Strategic Predictions/Recommendations Based Upon Threat

Identify Intelligence Gaps & Update Intel Requirements

Identify Future Perimeter Alerts and Blacklists

Develop New (Use) Business Cases

Update current CTI Repositories based upon new Tactical Intel

Identify Scenarios/Indicators for Future Mitigation

Distribute Reports/Process Feedback

Figure 4. **'Reporting' Workflow and Considerations**

# PART III - Appendices

## Appendix A – Relevant Terms and Glossary

**Audit log.** A chronological record of information system activities, including records of system accesses and operations performed in each period.

**Authentication.** Verifying the identity of a user, process, or device, often as a prerequisite to allowing access to resources in an information system.

**Availability.** Ensuring timely and reliable access to and use of information.

**Baseline Configuration.** A documented set of specifications for an information system, or a configuration item within a system, that has been formally reviewed and agreed on at a given point in time, and which can be changed only through change control procedures.

**Blacklisting.** The process used to identify: (i) software programs that are not authorized to execute on an information system; or (ii) prohibited websites.

**Confidentiality.** Preserving authorized restrictions on information access and disclosure, including means for protecting personal privacy and proprietary information.

**Configuration Management.** A collection of activities focused on establishing and maintaining the integrity of information technology products and information systems, through control of processes for initializing, changing, and monitoring the configurations of those products and systems throughout the system development life cycle.

**Controlled Unclassified Information (CUI/CDI).**

Information that law, regulation, or governmentwide policy requires to have safeguarding or disseminating controls, excluding information that is classified under Executive Order 13526, Classified National Security Information, December 29, 2009, or any predecessor or successor order, or the Atomic Energy Act of 1954, as amended.

| | |
|---|---|
| **Hardware.** | The physical components of an information system. |
| **Incident.** | An occurrence that actually or potentially jeopardizes the confidentiality, integrity, or availability of an information system or the information the system processes, stores, or transmits or that constitutes a violation or imminent threat of violation of security policies, security procedures, or acceptable use policies. |
| **Information Security.** | The protection of information and information systems from unauthorized access, use, disclosure, disruption, modification, or destruction to provide confidentiality, integrity, and availability. |
| **Information System.** | A discrete set of information resources organized for the collection, processing, maintenance, use, sharing, dissemination, or disposition of information. |
| **Information Technology.** | Any equipment or interconnected system or subsystem of equipment that is used in the automatic acquisition, storage, manipulation, management, movement, control, display, switching, interchange, transmission, or reception of data or information by the executive agency. It includes computers, ancillary equipment, software, firmware, and similar procedures, services (including support services), and related resources. |
| **Integrity.** | Guarding against improper information modification or destruction and includes ensuring information non-repudiation and authenticity. |
| **Internal Network.** | A network where: (i) the establishment, maintenance, and provisioning of security controls are under the direct control of organizational employees or contractors; or (ii) cryptographic encapsulation or similar security technology implemented between organization-controlled endpoints, provides the same effect (at least about confidentiality and integrity). |
| **Malicious Code.** | Software intended to perform an unauthorized process that will have adverse impact on the confidentiality, integrity, or availability of an information system. A virus, worm, Trojan horse, or other code-based entity that infects a host. Spyware and some forms of adware are also examples of malicious code. |

| | |
|---|---|
| **Media.** | Physical devices or writing surfaces including, but not limited to, magnetic tapes, optical disks, magnetic disks, and printouts (but not including display media) onto which information is recorded, stored, or printed within an information system. |
| **Mobile Code.** | Software programs or parts of programs obtained from remote information systems, transmitted across a network, and executed on a local information system without explicit installation or execution by the recipient. |
| **Mobile device.** | A portable computing device that: (i) has a small form factor such that it can easily be carried by a single individual; (ii) is designed to operate without a physical connection (e.g., wirelessly transmit or receive information); (iii) possesses local, nonremovable or removable data storage; and (iv) includes a self-contained power source. Mobile devices may also include voice communication capabilities, on-board sensors that allow the devices to capture information, and/or built-in features for synchronizing local data with remote locations. Examples include smartphones, tablets, and E-readers. |
| **Nonfederal Information System.** | An information system that does not meet the criteria for a federal information system. nonfederal organization. |
| **Network.** | Information system(s) implemented with a collection of interconnected components. Such components may include routers, hubs, cabling, telecommunications controllers, key distribution centers, and technical control devices. |
| **Privileged Account. user.** | An information system account with authorizations of a privileged |
| **Privileged User.** | A user that is authorized (and therefore, trusted) to perform security-relevant functions that ordinary users are not authorized to perform. |
| **Remote Access.** | Access to an organizational information system by a user (or a process acting on behalf of a user) communicating through an external network (e.g., the Internet). |

**Risk.** A measure of the extent to which an entity is threatened by a potential circumstance or event, and typically a function of: (i) the adverse impacts that would arise if the circumstance or event occurs; and (ii) the likelihood of occurrence. Information system-related security risks are those risks that arise from the loss of confidentiality, integrity, or availability of information or information systems and reflect the potential adverse impacts to organizational operations (including mission, functions, image, or reputation), organizational assets, individuals, other organizations, and the Nation.

**Sanitization.** Actions taken to render data written on media unrecoverable by both ordinary and, for some forms of sanitization, extraordinary means. Process to remove information from media such that data recovery is not possible. It includes removing all classified labels, markings, and activity logs.

**Security Control.** A safeguard or countermeasure prescribed for an information system or an organization designed to protect the confidentiality, integrity, and availability of its information and to meet a set of defined security requirements.

**Security Control Assessment.** The testing or evaluation of security controls to determine the extent to which the controls are implemented correctly, operating as intended, and producing the desired outcome with respect to meeting the security requirements for an information system or organization.

**Security Functions.** The hardware, software, and/or firmware of the information system responsible for enforcing the system security policy and supporting the isolation of code and data on which the protection is based.

**Threat.** Any circumstance or event with the potential to adversely impact organizational operations (including mission, functions, image, or reputation), organizational assets, individuals, other organizations, or the Nation through an information system via unauthorized access, destruction, disclosure, modification of information, and/or denial of service.

**Whitelisting.** The process used to identify: (i) software programs that are authorized to execute on an information system.

# Appendix B – Continuous Monitoring's Importance to the THP

*Continuous Monitoring (ConMon) is critical to any discussion of Hunt Team activities and operations. ConMon typically provides automated alerts to organizational IT personnel and is intended to provide real-time detection of threat activities. This paper better describes what ConMon is and how it would effectively be deployed in an IT environment. The description here is focused on the Eleven (11) NIST Security Domains and is intended as a primer on mainstream ConMon implementation.*

Cybersecurity is not about shortcuts. There are no easy solutions to years of leaders demurring their responsibility to address the growing threats in cyberspace. We hoped that the Office of Personnel Management (OPM) breach several years ago would herald the needed focus, energy and funding to quash the bad-guys. That has proven an empty hope where leaders have abrogated their responsibility to lead in cyberspace. The "holy grail" solution of ConMon has been the most misunderstood solution where too many shortcuts are perpetrated by numerous federal agencies and the private sector to create an illusion of success. This paper is specifically written to help leaders better understand what constitutes a true statement of: "we have continuous monitoring." This is not about shortcuts. This is about education, training, and understanding at the highest leadership levels that cybersecurity is not a technical issue, but a leadership issue.

The Committee on National Security Systems defines ConMon as: "[t]he processes implemented to maintain current security status for one or more information systems on which the operational mission of the enterprise depends," (CNSS, 2010). ConMon has been described as the holistic solution of end-to-end cybersecurity coverage and the answer to providing an effective global Risk Management (RM) solution. It promises the elimination of the 3-year recertification cycle that has been the bane of cybersecurity professionals.

For ConMon to become a reality for any agency, it must meet the measures and expectations as defined in National Institute of Standards and Technology (NIST) Special Publication (SP) 800-137, Information Security Continuous Monitoring for Federal Information Systems and Organizations. "Continuous monitoring has evolved as a best practice for managing risk on an ongoing basis," (SANS Institute, 2016); it is an instrument that supports effective, continual, and recurring RM assurances. For any agency to truly espouse it has attained full ConMon compliance, it must be able to coordinate all the described major elements as found in NIST SP 800-137.

ConMon is not just the passive visibility pieces, but also includes the active efforts of vulnerability scanning, threat alert, reduction, mitigation, or elimination of a dynamic

Information Technology (IT) environment. The Department of Homeland Security (DHS) has couched its approach to ConMon more holistically. Their program to protect government networks is more aptly called: "Continuous Diagnostics and Monitoring" or CDM and includes a need to react to an active network attacker. "The ability to make IT networks, end-points and applications visible; to identify malicious activity; and, to respond [emphasis added] immediately is critical to defending information systems and networks," (Sann, 2016).

Another description of ConMon can be found in NIST's CAESARS Framework Extension: An Enterprise Continuous Monitoring Technical Reference Model (Second Draft). It defines its essential characteristics within the concept of "Continuous Security Monitoring." It is described as a "...risk management approach to Cybersecurity that maintains a picture of an organization's security posture, provides visibility into assets, leverages use of automated data feeds, monitors effectiveness of security controls, and enables prioritization of remedies," (NIST, 2012); it must demonstrate visibility, data feeds, measures of effectiveness and allow for solutions. It provides another description of what should be demonstrated to ensure full ConMon designation under the NIST standard.

The government's Federal Risk and Authorization Management Program (Fed-RAMP) has defined similar ConMon goals. These objectives are all key outcomes of a successful ConMon implementation. Its "... goal[s]...[are] to provide: (i) operational visibility; (ii) annual self-attestations on security control implementations; (iii) managed change control; (iv) and attendance to incident response duties," (GSA, 2012). These objectives, while not explicit to NIST SP 800-37, are well-aligned with the desires of an effective and complete solution.

RMF creates the structure and documentation needs of ConMon; it represents the specific implementation and oversight of Information Security (IS) within an IT environment. It supports the general activity of RM within an agency. (See Figure 1 below). The RMF "... describes a disciplined and structured process that integrates information security and risk management activities into the system development life cycle," (NIST-B, 2011). RMF is the structure that both describes and relies upon ConMon as its risk oversight and effectiveness mechanism between IS and RM.

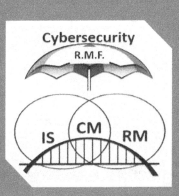

Figure 1. CM "bridges" Information Security and Risk Management

This article provides a conceptual framework to address how an agency would approach identifying a true ConMon solution through NIST SP 800-137. It discusses the additional need to align component requirements with the *"11 Security Automation Domains"* that are necessary to implement true ConMon. (See Figure 2 below). It is through the complete implementation and

Figure 2. The 11 Security Automation Domains (NIST, 2011)

integration with the other described components—See Figure 3 below--that an organization can correctly state it has achieved ConMon. incentives

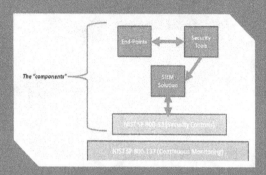

**Figure 3. The "Components" of an Effective Continuous Monitoring**

## Continuous Monitoring – First Generation

For ConMon to be effective and genuine, it must align end-point visibility with security monitoring tools. This includes security monitoring tools with connectivity to "end-points" such as laptops, desktops, servers, routers, firewalls, etc. Additionally, these must work with a highly integrated Security Information and Event Management (SIEM) device. The other "component" is a clear linkage between the end-points, security monitoring tools, and the SIEM appliance, working with the *Security Automation Domains* (See Figure 2). These would include, for example, the areas of malware detection, asset and event management. ConMon must first address these collective components to create a "First Generation" instantiation.

More specifically, a SIEM appliance provides the central core data processing capabilities to effectively coordinate all the inputs and outputs from across the IT enterprise. It manages the data integration and interpretation of all ConMon components. And, it provides the necessary visibility and intelligence for an active incident response capability.

***End-point devices must be persistently visible to the applicable security devices.*** Together, these parts must align with the respective security controls as described in NIST SP 800-53. The selected SIEM tool must be able to accept these inputs and analyze them against defined security policy settings, recurring vulnerability scans, signature-based threats, and heuristic/activity-based analyses to ensure the environment's security posture. The outputs of the SIEM must support the further visibility of the IT environment, conduct and disseminate vital intelligence, and alert leadership to any ongoing or imminent dangers. The expression above is designed to provide a conceptual representation of the cybersecurity professional attempting to ascertain effective ConMon implementation or to develop a complete ConMon answer for an agency.

Additionally, the SIEM must distribute data feeds in near-real time to analysts and key leaders. It provides for multi-level "dashboard" data streams and issues alert based upon prescribed policy settings. Once these base, First Generation functionalities are consistently aligning with the Security Automation Domains, then an organization can definitively express it meets the requirements of ConMon.

## End-Points

It is necessary to identify hardware and software configuration items that must be known and constantly traceable before implementing ConMon within an enterprise IT environment. End-point visibility is not the hardware devices, but the baseline software of each hardware device on the network.

Configuration Management is also a foundational requirement for any organization's security posture. Soundly implemented Configuration Management must be the basis of any complete CM implementation. At the beginning of any IS effort, cyber-professionals must know the current "as-is" hardware and software component state within the enterprise. End-points must be protected and monitored because they are the most valuable target for would-be hackers and cyber-thieves.

Configuration Management provides the baseline that establishes a means to identify potential compromise between the enterprise's end-points and the requisite security tools. "Organizations with a robust and effective [Configuration Management] process need to consider information security implications concerning the development and operation of information systems including hardware, software, applications, and documentation," (NIST-A, 2011).

The RMF requires the categorization of systems and data as high, moderate, or low regarding risk. The Federal Information Processing Standards (FIPS) Publication 199 methodology is typically used to establish data sensitivity levels in the federal government. FIPS 199 aids the cybersecurity professional in determining data protection standards of both end-points and the data stored in these respective parts. For example, a system that collects and retains sensitive data, such as financial information, requires a greater level of security. It is important that end-points are recognized as repositories of highly valued data to cyber-threats.

Further, cyber-security professionals must be constantly aware of the "...administrative and technological costs of offering a high degree of protection for all federal systems...," (Ross, Katzke, & Toth, 2005). This is not a matter of recognizing the physical end-point alone but the value and associated costs of the virtual data stored, monitored, and protected on a continual basis. FIPS 199 assists system owners in determining whether a higher level of protection is warranted, with higher associated costs, based upon an overall FIPS 199 evaluation.

## Security Tools

Security monitoring tools must identify in near-real time an active threat. Examples include anti-virus or anti-malware applications used to monitor network and end-point activities. Products like McAfee and Symantec provide enterprise capabilities that help to identify and reduce threats.

Other security tools would address in whole or part the remaining NIST Security

Automation Domains. These would include, for example, tools to provide asset visibility, vulnerability detection, patch management updates, etc. But it is also critical to recognize that even the best current security tools are not necessarily capable of defending against all attacks. New malware or zero-day attacks pose continual challenges to the cybersecurity workforce.

For example, DHS's EINSTEIN system would not have stopped the 2015 Office of Personnel Management breach. Even DHS's latest iteration of EINSTEIN, EINSTEIN 3, an advanced network monitoring and response system designed to protect federal governments' networks, would not have stopped that attack. "…EINSTEIN 3 would not have been able to catch a threat that [had] no known footprints, according to multiple industry experts," (Sternstein, 2015).

Not until there are a much greater integration and availability of cross-cutting intelligence and more capable security tools, can any single security tool ever be fully effective. The need for multiple security monitoring tools that provide "defense in depth" may be a better protective strategy. However, with multiple tools monitoring the same Security Automation Domains, such an approach will certainly increase the costs of maintaining a secure agency or C/U IT environment. A determination of Return on Investment (ROI) balanced against a well-defined threat risk scoring approach is further needed at all levels of the federal and C/U IT workspace.

## Security Controls

"Organizations are required to adequately mitigate the risk arising from the use of information and information systems in the execution of missions and C/U functions," (NIST, 2013). This is accomplished by the selection and implementation of NIST SP 800-53, Revision 4, described security controls. (See Figure 4 below). They are organized into eighteen families to address sub-set security areas such as access control, physical security, incident response, etc. The use of these controls is typically tailored to the security categorization by the respective system owner relying upon FIPS 199 categorization standards. A higher security categorization requires the greater implementation of these controls.

| ID | FAMILY | ID | FAMILY |
|----|--------|----|--------|
| AC | Access Control | MP | Media Protection |
| AT | Awareness and Training | PE | Physical and Environmental Protection |
| AU | Audit and Accountability | PL | Planning |
| CA | Security Assessment and Authorization | PS | Personnel Security |
| CM | Configuration Management | RA | Risk Assessment |
| CP | Contingency Planning | SA | System and Services Acquisition |
| IA | Identification and Authentication | SC | System and Communications Protection |
| IR | Incident Response | SI | System and Information Integrity |
| MA | Maintenance | PM | Program Management |

**Figure 4. Security Control Identifiers and Family Names, (NIST, 2013)**

## Security Information and Event Management (SIEM) Solutions

The SIEM tool plays a pivotal role in any viable "First Generation" implementation. Based on NIST and DHS guidance, an effective SIEM appliance must provide the following functionalities:

- "Aggregate data from "across a diverse set" of security tool sources;
- Analyze the multi-source data;
- Engage in explorations of data based on changing needs
- Make quantitative use of data for security (not just reporting) purposes including the development and use of risk scores; and
- Maintain actionable awareness of the changing security situation on a real-time basis," (Levinson, 2011).

"Effectiveness is further enhanced when the output is formatted to provide information that is specific, measurable, actionable, relevant, and timely," (NIST, 2011). The SIEM device is the vital core of a full solution that collects, analyzes, and alerts the cyber-professional of potential and actual dangers in their environment.

There are several major SIEM solutions that can effectively meet the requirements of NIST SP 800-137. They include products, for example, IBM® Security, Splunk®, and Hewlett Packard's® ArcSight® products.

For example, Logrhythm ® was highly rated in the 2014 SIEM evaluation. Logrhythm® provided network event monitoring and alerts of potential security compromises. The implementation of an enterprise-grade SIEM solution is necessary to meet growing cybersecurity requirements for auditing of security logs and capabilities to respond to cyber-incidents. SIEM products will continue to play a critical and evolving role in the demands for "...increased security and rapid response to events throughout the network," (McAfee® Foundstone Professional Services®, 2013). Improvements and upgrades of SIEM tools are critical to providing a more highly responsive capability for future generations of these appliances in the marketplace.

## Next Generations

Future generations of ConMon would include specific expanded capabilities and functionalities of the SIEM device. These second generation and beyond evolutions would be more effective solutions in future dynamic and hostile network environments. Such advancements might also include increased access to a greater pool of threat database signature repositories or more expansive heuristics that could identify active anomalies within a target network.

Another futuristic capability might include the use of Artificial Intelligence (AI). Improved capabilities of a SIEM appliance with AI augmentation would further enhance human threat analysis and provide for more automated responsiveness. "The concept of predictive analysis involves using statistical methods and decision tools that analyze current and historical data to make predictions about future events...," (SANS Institute). The next generation would boost human response times and abilities to defend against attacks in a matter of milli-seconds vice hours.

Finally, in describing the next generations of ConMon, it is not only imperative to expand data, informational and intelligence inputs for new and more capable SIEM products, but that input and corresponding data sets must also be fully vetted for completeness and accuracy. Increased access to signature and heuristic activity-based analysis databases would provide greater risk reduction. Greater support from private industry and the Intelligence Community would also be major improvements for Agencies that are constantly struggling against a more-capable and better-resourced threat.

ConMon will not be a reality until vendors and agencies can integrate the right people, processes, and technologies. "Security needs to be positioned as an enabler of the organization—it must take its place alongside human resources, financial resources, sound C/U processes and strategies, information technology, and intellectual capital as the elements of success for accomplishing the mission," (Caralli, 2004). ConMon is not just a technical solution. It requires capable organizations with trained personnel, creating effective policies and procedures with the requisite technologies to stay ahead of the growing threats in cyberspace.

Figure 6 below provides a graphic depiction of what ConMon components are needed to create a holistic NIST SP 800-137-compliant solution; this demonstrates the First-Generation representation. There are numerous vendors describing that they have the "holy grail" solution, but until they can prove they meet this description in total, it is unlikely they have a complete implementation of a thorough ConMon solution yet.

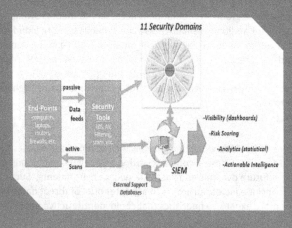

Figure 6. First Generation Continuous Monitoring

# References for "Continuous Monitoring and the THP"

Balakrishnan, B. (2015, October 6). *Insider Threat Mitigation Guidance* . Retrieved from SANS Institute Infosec Reading Room: https://www.sans.org/reading-room/whitepapers/monitoring/insider-threat-mitigation-guidance-36307

Caralli, R. A. (2004, December). *Managing Enterprise Security (CMU/SEI-2004-TN-046)*. Retrieved from Software Engineering Institute: http://www.sei.cmu.edu/reports/04tn046.pdf

Committee on National Security Systems. (2010, April 26). *National Information Assurance (IA) Glossary*. Retrieved from National Counterintelligence & Security Center: http://www.ncsc.gov/nittf/docs/CNSSI-4009_National_Information_Assurance.pdf

Department of Defense. (2014, March 12). *DOD Instructions 8510.01: Risk Management Framework (RMF) for DoD Information Technology (IT)*. Retrieved from Defense Technical Information Center (DTIC): http://www.dtic.mil/whs/directives/corres/pdf/851001_2014.pdf

GSA. (2012, January 27). *Continuous Monitoring Strategy & Guide, v1.1*. Retrieved from General Services Administration: http://www.gsa.gov/graphics/staffoffices/Continuous_Monitoring_Strategy_Guide_072712.pdf

Joint Medical Logistics Functional Development Center. (2015). JMLFDC Continuous Monitoring Strategy Plan and Procedure. Ft Detrick, MD.

Kavanagh, K. M., Nicolett, M., & Rochford, O. (2014, June 25). *Magic Quadrant for Security Information and Event Management*. Retrieved from Gartner: http://www.gartner.com/technology/reprints.do?id=1-1W8AO4W&ct=140627&st=sb&mkt_tok=3RkMMJWWfF9wsRolsqrJcO%2FhmjTEU5z17u8lWa%2BOgYkz2EFye%2BLIHETpodcMTcVkNb%2FYDBceEJhqyQJxPr3FKdANz8JpRhnqAA%3D%3D

Kolenko, M. M. (2016, February 18). *SPECIAL-The Human Element of Cybersecurity*. Retrieved from Homeland Security Today.US: http://www.hstoday.us/briefings/industry-news/single-article/special-the-human-element-of-cybersecurity/54008efd46e93863f54db0f7352dde2c.html

Levinson, B. (2011, October). *Federal Cybersecurity Best Practices Study: Information Security Continuous Monitoring*. Retrieved from Center for Regulatory Effectiveness: http://www.thecre.com/fisma/wp-content/uploads/2011/10/Federal-Cybersecurity-Best-Practice.ISCM_2.pdf

McAfee® Foundstone® Professional Services. (2013). *McAfee*. Retrieved from White Paper: Creating and Maintaining a SOC: http://www.mcafee.com/us/resources/white-papers/foundstone/wp-creating-maintaining-soc.pdf

NIST. (2011-A, August). *NIST SP 800-128: Guide for Security-Focused Configuration Management of Information Systems*. Retrieved from NIST Computer Security Resource Center: http://csrc.nist.gov/publications/nistpubs/800-128/sp800-128.pdf

NIST. (2011-B, September). *Special Publication 800-137: Information Security Continuous Monitoring (ISCM) for Federal Information Systems and Organizations*. Retrieved from NIST Computer

Security Resource Center: http://csrc.nist.gov/publications/nistpubs/800-137/SP800-137-Final.pdf

NIST. (2012, January). *NIST Interagency Report 7756: CAESARS Framework Extension: An Enterprise Continuous Monitoring Technical Reference Model (Second Draft),* . Retrieved from NIST Computer Resource Security Center: http://csrc.nist.gov/publications/drafts/nistir-7756/Draft-NISTIR-7756_second-public-draft.pdf

NIST. (2013, April). *NIST SP 800-53, Rev 4: Security and Privacy Controls for Federal Information Systems* . Retrieved from NIST: http://nvlpubs.nist.gov/nistpubs/SpecialPublications/NIST.SP.800-53r4.pdf

Ross, R., Katzke, S., & Toth, P. (2005, October 17). *The New FISMA Standards and Guidelines Changing the Dynamic of Information Security for the Federal Government.* Retrieved from Information Technology Promotion Agency of Japan: https://www.ipa.go.jp/files/000015362.pdf

Sann, W. (2016, January 8). *The Key Missing Piece of Your Cyber Strategy? Visibility.* Retrieved from Nextgov: http://www.nextgov.com/technology-news/tech-insider/2016/01/key-missing-element-your-cyber-strategy-visibility/124974/

SANS Institute. (2016, March 6). *Beyond Continuous Monitoring: Threat Modeling for Real-time Response.* Retrieved from SANS Institute: http://www.sans.org/reading-room/whitepapers/analyst/continuous-monitoring-threat-modeling-real-time-response-35185

Sternstein, A. (2015, January 6). *OPM Hackers Skirted Cutting-Edge Intrusion Detection System, Official Says* . Retrieved from Nextgov: http://www.nextgov.com/cybersecurity/2015/06/opm-hackers-skirted-cutting-edge-interior-intrusion-detection-official-says/114649/

## Appendix C -- Can the Human "Poet" Bring Value to Predictive Analysis?

From the time we are children through adulthood we are reminded that that which cannot be measured cannot be properly managed. (This is the core of why metrics must be a vital part of THP). The United States Congress, for example, repeatedly calls for better measurements and metrics; however, they do not appear to subsequently predict or at least foresee the next financial crisis, political coup or cybersecurity attack with these numbers alone. It is not just the absence of such data, but the lack of employment of the qualitative strengths of the human element.

The predictive forecasting and modeling community recognize the value that humans bring to the field of data analytics. As Hubbard and Seiersen (2016) state: "...if the primary concern about using probabilistic methods is the lack of data, then you also lack the data to use non-quantitative methods" (p. 38). The "human element" is that derived and non-quantitative component that is needed.

There are several reasons the often biased, irrational, and poetic human will continue to contribute to the quality of the quantitative. This includes the value of the individual subject matter expert, the collective synergy of a larger sample of experts, and the innate innovativeness of man attempting to solve problems and reject the status quo. Humans do not detract from the calculations but provide their own unique recognition and context to both the inputs and the results.

Hubbard & Seiersen (2016) and Tetlock & Gardner (2016) identify the importance of the "calibrated" subject matter expert to improve the state of predictive analysis. Such an individual is not only proficient in their field, but also has been trained to understand a significant facet of quantitative measurement: uncertainty. These individuals are described by Tetlock (2016) as the "superforecasters." Silver (2012) recognizes that forecasting is not about absolute mathemetical precision, but the acknowledgement of the importance of knowing that "[w]e must become more comfortable with probability **and** [emphasis added] uncertainty" (p. 15); the individual understands the role of uncertainty where the mathematical equation or model does not. It is this uncertainty that helps others understand the expected deviation by the superforecaster, specifically, as the norm and not the exception to real accuracy.

It is also the collective nature of human beings attempting to solve problems that continues to contribute to better predictive analytic outcomes. In 1906, the British Scientist, Sir Francis Galton, conducted an experiment where he had several hundred individuals attempt to determine the final weight of a slaughtered cow. The result was greater accuracy from the collective crowd. With remarkable precision, the average weight guessed by the participants was 1197 pounds, and in fact, the actual weight was 1198 pounds (Tetlock & Gardner, 2016). It is this type of "crowd sourcing" effect that demonstrates the informed and knowledgeable average of all guesses (or, predictions) culminated into a final and near accurate answer. It is this collective "hive mind" that shows how the accumulation of human knowledge can be brought together to directly enhance the precision of the result.

Additionally, Christakis and Fowler (2009) recognize that individually humans are an important component of quantified and predictive outcomes, but even greater outcomes are possible jointly. "...[C]hallenges require us to recognize that although human beings are individually powerful, we must act together to achieve what we could not accomplish on our own" (p. 304). The more knowledgeable experts contributing to a predictive analytical formula or algorithm will more likely contribute to greater accuracy less any identified uncertainty.

In the book, *Moneyball* (Lewis, 2004), Billy Beane, the coach of the Oakland A's baseball team, successfully employed the rigors of data analysis and statistics to propel his team to its historical twenty game winning streak where it was one of the worst ranked teams at the time (Thum, 2012). The challenges were many, but he knew that following the old models of human instinct, hunches, and guess work in selecting the best players was not going to solve his biggest problem—not having the larger payrolls that other big-league teams had to recruit the "best" players (Lewis, 2004).

Beane also identified that baseball scouting "...was at roughly the same stage of development in the twenty-first century as professional medicine was in the eighteenth" (Lewis, 2004, p. 17). His recruiting of Paul DePodesta, a Harvard graduate with a love of math, statistics, and baseball was a recognition that there was a need for innovation; an innovation that riled his own internal scouting staff (Lewis, 2004). It was his ultimate and revolutionary acknowledgment of the mathematical approaches brought by DePodesta that was so effective for the improvement of the Oakland A's successful winning on the playing field.

The human element in the form of the Cyber Analyst (CyA) will always be a vital part of data analytical and predictive improvements. With the exponential growth and access to data and the power of the fledgling data science community, it will bring needed value to the development of such analyses. Future predictive analytic progress will rely upon the unique abilities man presents, and it will directly result in better forecasts. These better forecasts will be a consequence of man's ability to grow and improve the very state of his own world around him.

**References for "Can the Human Poet Bring Value to Predictive Analysis?"**

Christakis, N., & Fowler, J. (2009). *Connected; The surprising power of our social networks and how they shape our lives.* New York: Little, Brown & Company.

Hubbard, D., & Seiersen, R. (2016). *How to measure anything in cybersecurity risk.* Hoboken, NJ: John wiley & sons.

Lewis, M. (2004). *Moneyball: The art of winning an unfair game.* New York: WW Norton & Company.

Silver, N. (2012). *The signal and the noise: Why so many predictions fail--but some don't.* New York: Penguin.

Tetlock, P., & Gardner, D. (2016). *Superforecasting: The art and science of prediction.* New York: Random House.

Thum, W. (2012, August 19). *Ten years later: The A's 20-game winning streak, Scott Hatteberg, and Moneyball.* Retrieved from SBNATION.com: https://www.sbnation.com/2012/8/19/3250200/ten-year-anniversary-athletics-20-game-winning-streak-hatteberg-moneyball

# About the Author

Mr. Russo is the former Senior Information Security Engineer within the Department of Defense's (DOD) F-35 Joint Strike Fighter program. He has an extensive background in cybersecurity and is an expert in the Risk Management Framework (RMF) and DOD Instruction 8510 which implements RMF throughout the DOD and the federal government. He holds both a Certified Information Systems Security Professional (CISSP) certification and a CISSP in information security architecture (ISSAP). He holds a 2017 certification as a Chief Information Security Officer (CISO) from the National Defense University, Washington, DC. He retired from the US Army Reserves in 2012 as the Senior Intelligence Officer.

He is the former CISO at the Department of Education wherein 2016 he led the effort to close over 95% of the outstanding US Congressional and Inspector General cybersecurity shortfall weaknesses spanning as far back as five years.

Mr. Russo is the former Senior Cybersecurity Engineer supporting the Joint Medical Logistics Development Functional Center of the Defense Health Agency (DHA) at Fort Detrick, MD. He led a team of engineering and cybersecurity professionals protecting five major Medical Logistics systems supporting over 200 DOD Medical Treatment Facilities around the globe.

In 2011, Mr. Russo was certified by the Office of Personnel Management as a graduate of the Senior Executive Service Candidate program.

From 2009 through 2011, Mr. Russo was the Chief Technology Officer at the Small Business Administration (SBA). He led a team of over 100 IT professionals in supporting an intercontinental Enterprise IT infrastructure and security operations spanning 12-time zones; he deployed cutting-edge technologies to enhance SBA's business and information sharing operations supporting the small business community.     Mr. Russo was the first-ever Program Executive Officer (PEO)/Senior Program Manager in the Office of Intelligence & Analysis at Headquarters, Department of Homeland Security (DHS), Washington, DC. Mr. Russo was responsible for the development and deployment of secure Information and Intelligence support systems for OI&A to include software applications and systems to enhance the DHS mission. He was responsible for the program management development lifecycle during his tenure at DHS.

He holds a Master of Science from the National Defense University in Government Information Leadership with a concentration in Cybersecurity and a Bachelor of Arts in Political Science with a minor in Russian Studies from Lehigh University. He holds Level III Defense Acquisition certification in Program Management, Information Technology, and Systems Engineering. He has been a member of the DOD Acquisition Corps since 2001.

## System Security Plan (SSP) Template & Workbook NIST-based

https://www.amazon.com/System-Security-Plan-Template-Workbook-ebook/dp/B07BCY41D2/ref=sr_1_1?ie=UTF8&qid=1523490730&sr=8-1&keywords=system+security+plan

"SSP" is designed to provide more specific, direction and guidance on completing the core NIST 800-171 artifact, the System Security Plan (SSP). This is part of a ongoing series of support documents being developed to address the recent changes and requirements levied by the Federal Government on contractors wishing to do business with the government. The intent of these supplements is to provide immediate and valuable information so business owners and their Information Technology (IT) staff need. The changes are coming rapidly for cybersecurity contract requirements. Are you ready? We plan to be ahead of the curve with you with high-quality books that can provide immediate support to the ever-growing challenges of cyber-threats to the Government and your business.

### The Agile/Security Development Life Cycle (A/SDLC): Integrating Security Functionality into the SDLC ~SECOND EDITION (2019)

https://www.amazon.com/Agile-Security-Development-Life-Cycle/dp/1794490574/ref=tmm_pap_swatch_0?_encoding=UTF8&qid=1549597464&sr=8-4-fkmr2

In this SECOND EDITION of THE AGILE SECURITY DEVELOPMENT LIFE CYCLE (A/SDLC) we expand and include new information to improve the concept of "Agile Cyber." We further discuss the need for a Security Traceability Requirements Matrix (SecRTM) and the need to know where all data elements are located throughout your IT environment to include Cloud storage and repository locations. The author continues his focus upon ongoing shortfalls and failures of "Secure System Development." The author seeks to use his over 25 years in the public and private sector program management and cybersecurity to create a solution. This book provides the first-ever integrated operational-security process to enhance the readers understanding of why systems are so poorly secured. Why we as a nation have missed the mark in cybersecurity? Why nation-states and hackers are successful daily? This book also describes the two major mainstream "agile" NIST frameworks that can be employed, and how to use them effectively under a Risk Management approach. We may be losing "battles, " but may be its time we truly commit to winning the cyber-war.